great songs... of broadway

edited by **milton okun**

ISBN 1-57560-658-5

Visit our website at www.cherrylane.com

Introduction: The American Musical Theater and Popular Song

Play, sing, or hum the opening bars of "There's No Business Like Show Business" and you can be sure it will be identified as a "show tune." The repeated, bracing rhythm and rushing, ascending scales capture the dynamism and vitality of Broadway like no other song from the American musical theater. In fact, you could justifiably change the words to "There's No Show Tune Like This Show Tune" and be right on the mark (though off on the lyrics!).

Irving Berlin's optimistic paean to showbiz was written for his 1946 hit *Annie Get Your Gun,* smack in the midst of one of Broadway's most successful decades. A seemingly endless array of musicals flowed from America's legendary composers and lyricists, with Berlin, Cole Porter, Richard Rodgers, Lorenz Hart, and Oscar Hammerstein just the top of the pack. Their songs leapt from the Broadway stage to radio, recordings, sheet music and film, growing into a multi-million dollar business. Broadway songs of the 1940s were the popular music of their day and offered something for everyone: the ironic, sophisticated love song (*Pal Joey:* "Bewitched, Bothered and Bewildered"); ardent, operetta-tinged ballads (*Carousel:* "If I Loved You"); zesty production numbers (*Kiss Me, Kate:* "Another Op'nin', Another Show") and, rare qualities in today's popular music, comfort, optimism and hope (*Oklahoma!:* "Oh, What a Beautiful Mornin'").

Whatever the tempo or subject, these songs shared certain traits: brief, distinctly memorable melodies (the "tunes"); clear, succinct, often extremely clever lyrics (the opening of "Bewitched": "I'm wild again, beguiled again, a simpering, whimpering child again"); and a basic 32-bar structure that allowed enough repetition to clarify the musical and textual point without belaboring it. As they all have a particular dramatic function, they are really more than just good tunes; these are *theater songs*, meant to entertain at the same time as they illuminate the action, mood, and characters—and move the plot along.

Thus the opening song of *Oklahoma!*, "Oh, What a Beautiful Mornin'," with its gentle waltz time and lyrics evoking a verdant, ever-expanding American countryside ("The corn is as high as an elephant's eye/And it looks like it's climbin' clear up to the sky") set a mood of joyous optimism and hope that dominates the show. In "Hello, Young Lovers," from *The King and I*, a stately waltz underscores the gracious and eminently proper Anna, the widowed English governess employed by the King of Siam. But when she remembers the thrill of love ("I know how it feels to have wings on your heels") her melody soars as she transports the audience to the realm of her heart. It's a brief, intimate moment, but one that stays in the memory long after the show is over.

Such intimate moments were a hallmark of the Broadway musical, and many became popular hits in the 1950s and 1960s including "If Ever I Would Leave You," "The Impossible Dream," and "People" (Barbra Streisand's first Top Ten single). At the opposite end of the Broadway musical spectrum are the big production numbers that put main characters in a public setting and colorfully evoke the period, be it bawdy, cockney London ("I'm Getting Married in the Morning"), small town USA ("Seventy Six Trombones"), or gaslight New York ("Hello, Dolly!").

These solo and ensemble turns provide the emotional and dramatic high points of the journey that makes up a Broadway musical. It's a journey that usually says "Let Me Entertain You" (to quote the opening song from *Gypsy*), but not always. Few "show tunes" have the exuberant rush of "Cabaret," for example, but the song is in marked contrast to the dark tone of the show, which chronicles the rise of the Nazis in pre-war Berlin. And the slow strut of "One" from *A Chorus Line* sounds like a lead-in to a show-stopping production number for a leading lady, but no star ever appears. The song, like the show, is about the singer/dancers who make up the chorus, the drudgery, sweat, and sometimes broken dreams they go through to make the star look glamorous.

A Chorus Line had a pop hit with "What I Did for Love" in 1975, but by that time a Broadway crossover hit was unusual. With the ascension of rock, television, and, later, MTV into pop culture, very few hit songs came from musicals, and to many young people the Broadway musical seemed "old hat." Some scores, like that of *Jekyll & Hyde*, attempt to meld the two worlds with anthems and ballads of unabashed emotionalism ("This Is the Moment," "Someone Like You"), while the English musicals *Les Misérables, Miss Saigon* and the works of Andrew Lloyd Webber (*Jesus Christ Superstar, Evita, Cats, The Phantom of the Opera*) are a unique amalgam of pop, opera, and spectacle that sound and feel very different from the traditional Broadway show.

Successful as these shows were, others continued the Broadway tradition with music in a direct line from the classics of the 1940s and 1950s. The score of *Nine* abounds in songs that characterize the suave, passionate film director Guido Contini ("Only with You") and the women whose lives are indelibly altered by him ("Simple," "Unusual Way"). And in the unusual extended opening sequence of *Titanic—The Musical*, the excitement of the passengers ("I Must Get on That Ship"), the majesty of the ship, and the symbolic importance of the maiden voyage are captured in a series of connected songs that culminate in the triumphant "Godspeed Titanic."

Broadway also saw a resurgence of traditional musical comedy at the turn of the new century, often referencing earlier eras. *Thoroughly Modern Millie* transports us to the Roaring Twenties ("Thoroughly Modern Millie"), while every song in *The Producers* nostalgically (and often hysterically) nods to the 1950s musical ("'Til Him").

And then there's Stephen Sondheim, the most active composer/lyricist on Broadway of the last half century. His songs pay reverence to the style he grew up with, while exploring psychological depths only hinted at by his predecessors. He is, as the aged, but ever-youthful showgirl in *Follies*, "just a Broadway Baby."

As are all of us who cherish the Great Songs of Broadway.

—Dan Rosenbaum

Dan Rosenbaum has written articles for *Opera News, Music Alive!*, and other publications.

CONTENTS

from KISS ME, KATE

Another Op'nin', Another Show

Words and Music by Cole Porter

F
F♯dim7
C7
chance for stage - folks to say "Hel - lo," An -
F
D7♭9
4fr
Gm7♭5
5fr
C13
2fr
oth - er op' - nin' of an - oth - er
F
show. An - oth - er job that you hope, at last,
F6
Will make your fu - ture for -

F
get your past, An - oth - er pain
F♯dim7
C7
F
D7♭9
4 fr
where the ul - cers grow, An - oth - er op' -
Gm7♭5
5 fr
C13
2 fr
F
E7
- nin' of an - oth - er show!
Am
Am6
5 fr
E
F♯m7
Edim/G
E7/G♯
E7
Four weeks, you re - hearse and re - hearse,

Am
Am6
5 fr
F/D♯
Am/E
F7
E
E7
Three weeks, and it could - n't be worse,
Am
Am6
5fr
D7
C/E
F♯m7♭5
4fr
G
One week, will it ev - er be right?
C
C/B
C/B♭
C/A
D7
G7♯5
C
Then out of the hat it's that big first night!
C7
F
The o - ver - ture is a -

F6
bout to start, You cross your fin -
F
- gers and hold your heart, It's cur - tain time
F♯dim7
C7
and a - way we go, An -
F
D7♭5
Gm7♭5
5 fr
C13
2 fr
F
oth - er op' - nin' of an - oth - er show.
sfz

from SOUTH PACIFIC

Bali Ha'i

Lyrics by Oscar Hammerstein II
Music by Richard Rodgers

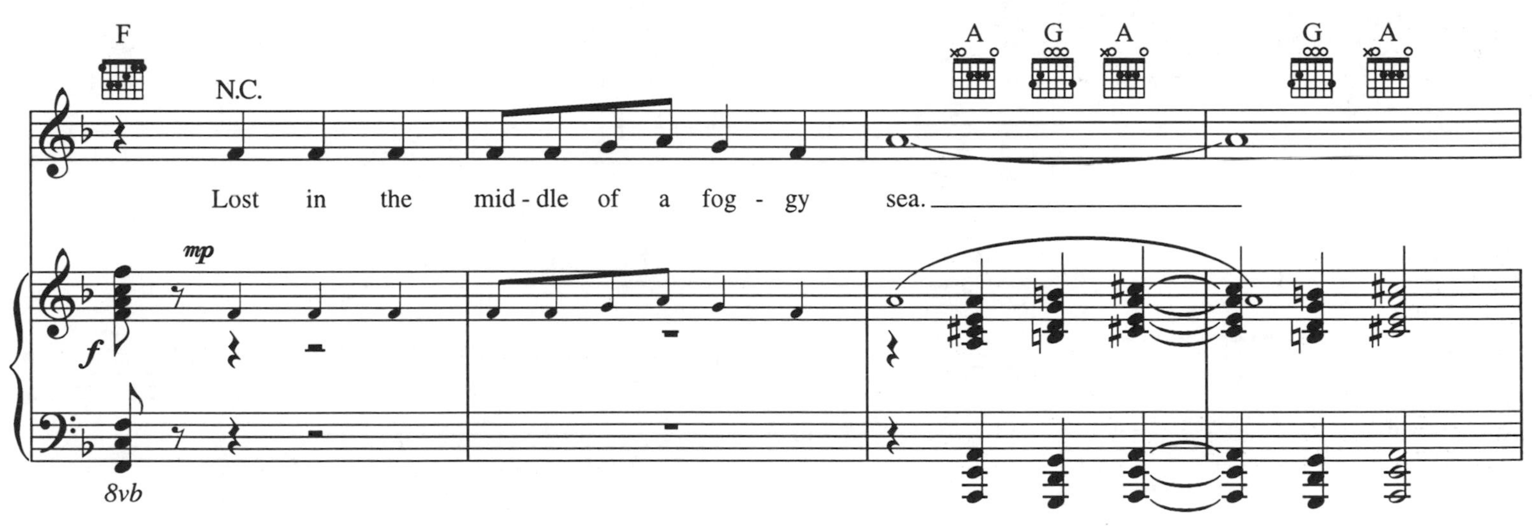

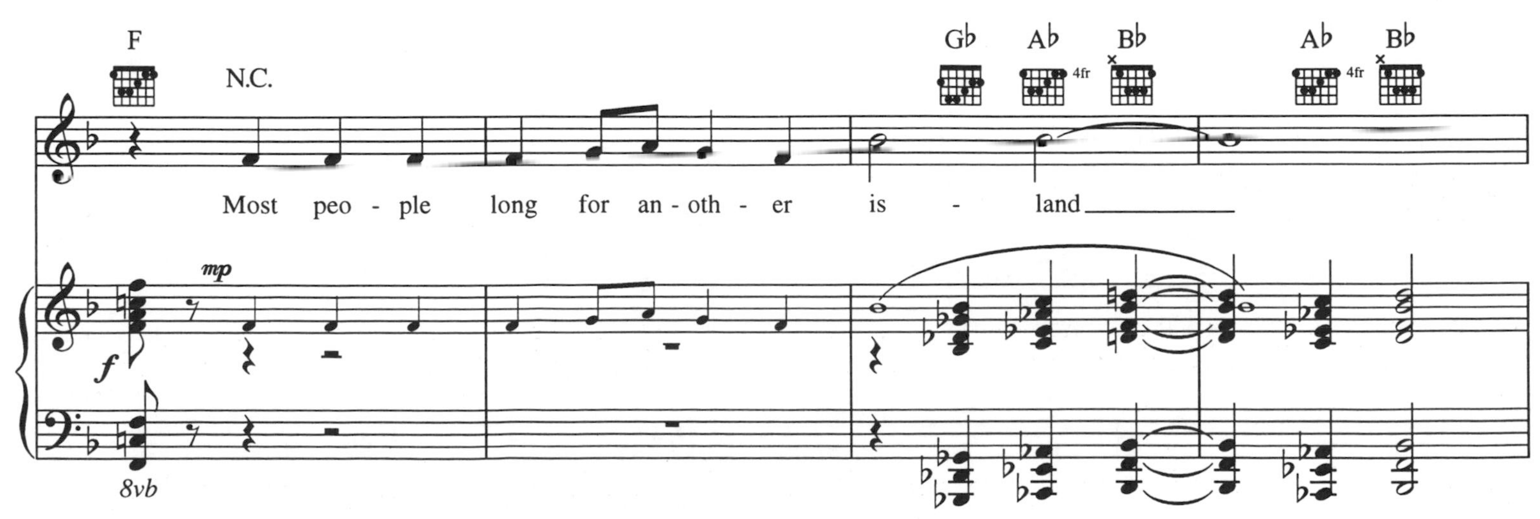

Gm7
C
C7
One where they know they would like to be.
Ba - li
rit.
8vb
Refrain (slowly)
Fdim
F
Ha'i may call you an - y night, An - y day. In your
p-mf
E/F
Db7/F
C7
heart you'll hear it call you: "Come a - way, Come a - way." Ba - li
Ha'i will whis - per On the wind of the sea: "Here am

E/F
D♭7/F
F
D♭7/F
C7
F
I, Your spe - cial is - land! Come to me, come to me!" Your
B♭
B♭+
own spe - cial hopes, Your own spe - cial dreams
mf
Gm
3fr
B♭m/D♭
C7
Bloom on the hill - side And shine in the streams. If you
mp
Fdim
F
Fdim
F
try, You'll find me, Where the sky Meets the sea. "Here am

E/F
D♭7/F
F
D♭7/F
C7
I, Your spe - cial is - land! Come to me, Come to
F7
B♭
C9
me!" Ba - li Ha'i, Ba - li Ha'i, Ba - li
cresc.
1
F6
Edim7/F
Dm/F
Ha'i! Some day you'll see me,
mf
mp
Edim7/F
Dm/F
Gdim7/F
3fr
Float - ing in the sun - shine, My head stick - ing out From a low - fly - ing

F6
Gdim7/F
Dm/F
3fr
cloud.
You'll hear me call you,
Gdim7/F
Dm/F
G♭
A♭
B♭
A♭
B♭
4fr
Sing - ing through the sun - shine,
Sweet and clear as can
D♭
E♭
F
be.
"Come to me, Here am I, come to
mf
cresc.
C7
2 F6
me!"
Ba - li Ha'i!
cresc.
f
f

from PAL JOEY

Bewitched

Words by Lorenz Hart
Music by Richard Rodgers

Dm7 G7 Cmaj7 C6 Dm7 G7
Since this half - pint im - i - ta - tion, Put me on the blink. I'm
rit.
Slowly
C G7/D C/E C+/E
wild a - gain, be - guiled a - gain, a sim - per - ing, whim - per - ing
p a tempo
F Ddim7 C/E D7 G7 A7
child a - gain, Be - witched, both - ered and be - wil - dered am
Dm G7 C G7/D
I. Could - n't sleep, and would - n't sleep, When
mf
p

C/E
C+/E
F
Ddim7
C/E
D7
love came and told me I should - n't sleep, Be - witched, both - ered and be -
G7
C7
F
A7
wil - dered am I.
mp
Dm
Dm7
Am
Lost my heart, but what of it? He is cold, I a -
Dm7
G7
Dm7/G
G7
gree, He can laugh, but I love it, Al - though the

Em7
E♭dim7
Dm7
G7
C
laugh's on me. I'll sing to him, each
mf
p
G7/D
C/E
C+/E
F
Ddim7
spring to him, And long for the day when I'll cling to him, Be -
C/E
D7
G9
1
C
Am
witched, both - ered and be - wil - dered am I.
Dm7
G7
2
C
F
C6
I'm I.
sf

from JEKYLL & HYDE

Bring On The Men

Words by Leslie Bricusse
Music by Frank Wildhorn

C♯m
G♯7
C♯madd9
learn - ing.
A girl a - lone, all
eas - y.
So man - y men, so
F♯m6
on her own, must try to have a heart of stone. So
lit - tle time; I want 'em all, is that a crime? "No!" I
D♯m7♭5
G♯7sus4
G♯7
C♯m
I try not to make it known, my yearn - ing.
don't know why they say that I'm too eas - y.
F♯m9
I try to show I have no need; I
They make me laugh, they make me cry; they

D♯m7♭5
G♯7sus4
G♯7
real - ly do, I don't suc - ceed! So let's bring
make me sick, so God knows why we say: Bring
Bright cut time (Tempo II)
C♯m
F♯m
on the men and let the fun be - gin; a lit - tle
mf
B
A/E
E
G♯7♭9
G♯7
touch of sin, why wait an - oth - er min - ute?
C♯m
F♯m
Step this way; it's time for us to play. They say we

D♯m7♭5
G♯sus4
may not pass this way a - gain, so let's waste no more
1.
Tempo I
G♯
C♯m
G♯7
time. Bring on the men! I
2.
G♯
C♯m
time. Bring on the men! They break your
F♯m
B
G♯m7
heart, they steal your soul,

C♯m
F♯m
B7
Esus4
E
take you a - part, and yet they some - how
C♯7♯5
C♯7
F♯m
B
G♯m7
make you whole. So what's their game?
Slowly
C♯m
F♯m
I sup - pose a rose by an - y oth - er name, the
rit.
D♯m7♭5
G♯sus4
G♯
Tempo II
per - fume and the prick's the same.

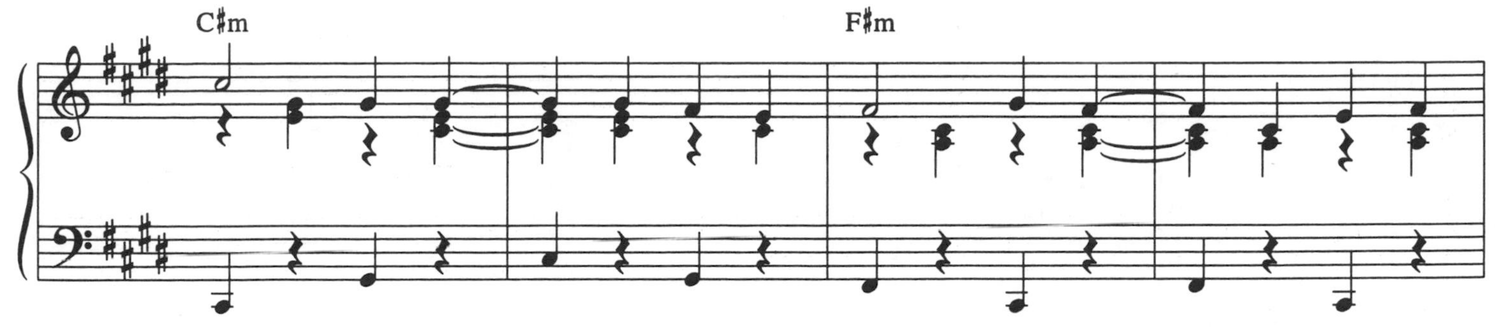
C♯m
F♯m

B
A/E
E
G♯7♭9
G♯7
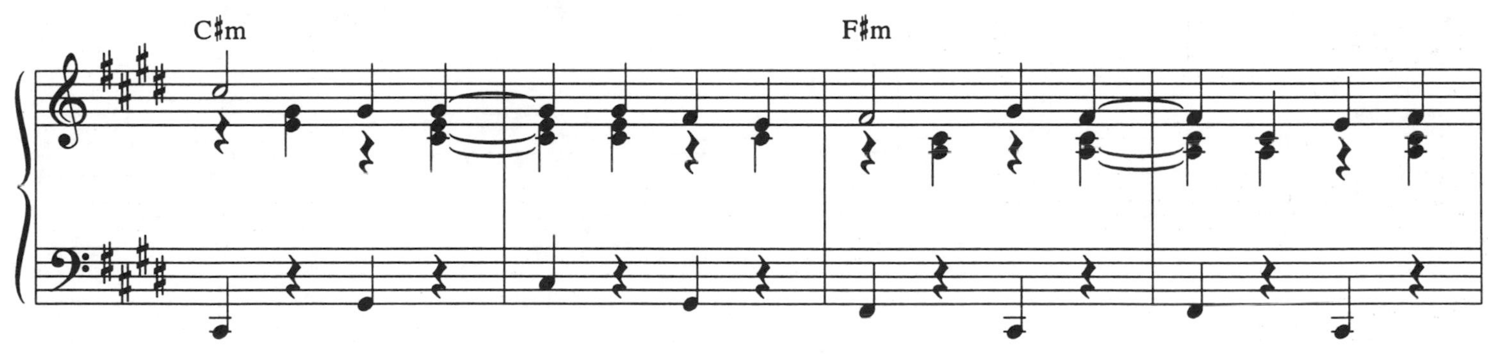
C♯m
F♯m

D♯m7♭5
G♯7sus4
G♯7

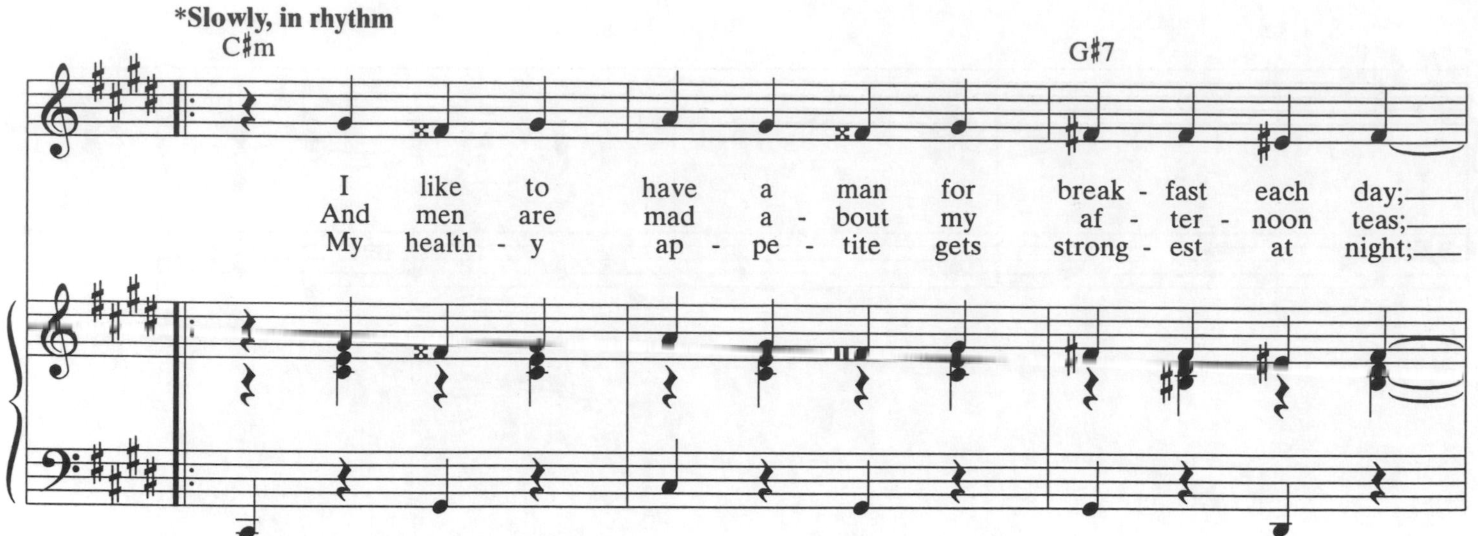

* This section is played three times: Slow, Moderately, and Fast (Tempo II).

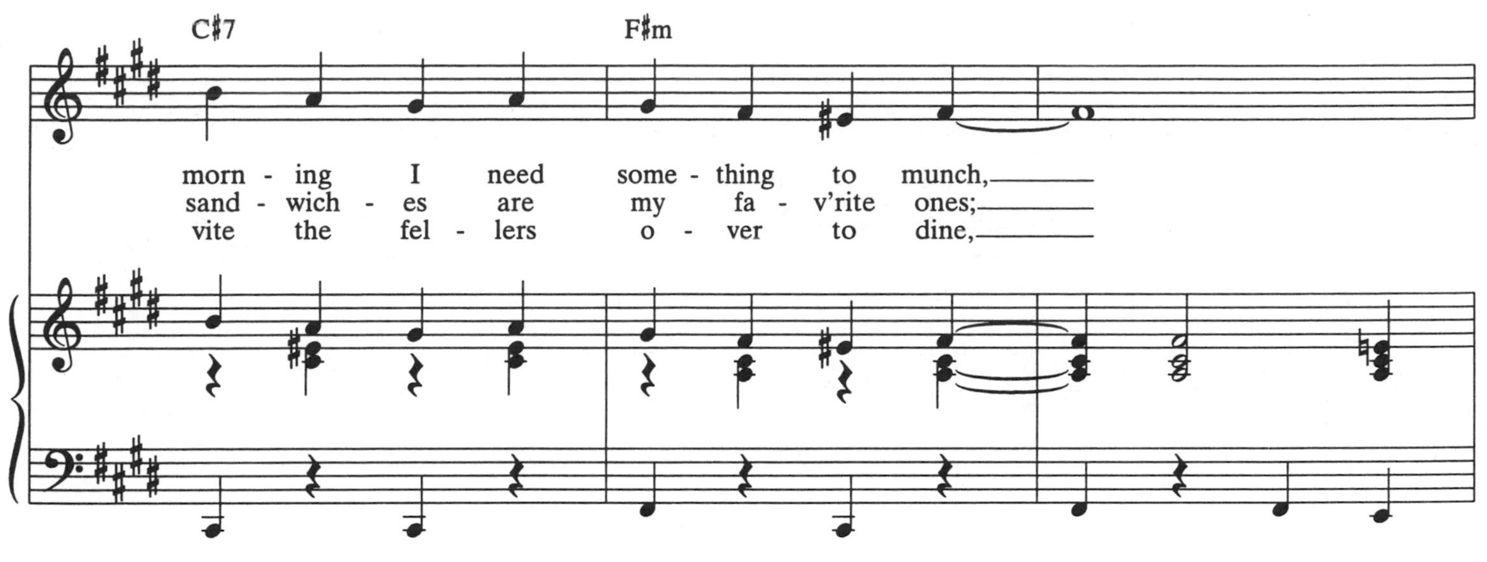
C♯7
F♯m
morn - ing I need some - thing to munch,
sand - wich - es are my fa - v'rite ones;
vite the fel - lers o - ver to dine,

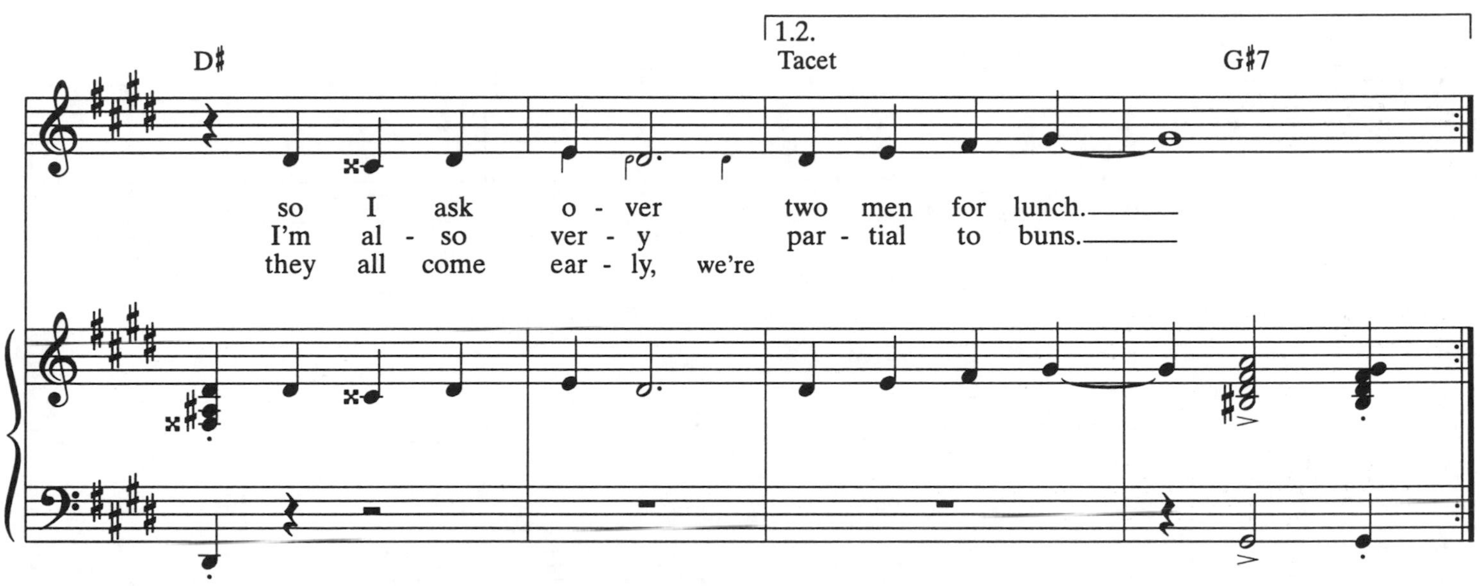
D♯
1.2.
Tacet
G♯7
so I ask o - ver two men for lunch.
I'm al - so ver - y par - tial to buns.
they all come ear - ly, we're

3.
Tacet
C♯m
A7
in bed by nine!
So let's bring

Dm
Gm
on the men, and let the fun be - gin;
f
C
a lit - tle touch of sin, why wait an -
B♭/F
F
A7♭9
A7
Dm
oth - er min - ute? Step this way,
Gm
it's time for us to play. They say we

Em7♭5
Asus4
may not pass this way a - gain, so let's waste no more
molto rit.
A
Dm
Gm
Dm
time. Bring on the men!
a tempo
Dm
Dm
Dm
Gm
Dm
Gm
Dm
8vb

from FOLLIES

Broadway Baby

Words and Music by Stephen Sondheim

Broad-way Ba - by,
Learn-ing how to sing and dance,
Wait-ing for that one big chance to be in a show.
p
mf
Gee, I'd like to be on some mar - quee, All twin - kling lights, a
3
spark to pierce the dark From Bat-t'ry Park to Wash - ing-ton Heights.

Some day, may - be,
All my dreams will be re - paid.
Hell, I'd e - ven play the maid
to be in a
show!
Say, Mis - ter Pro - duc - er,
I'm talk - ing to you, sir.
I don't need a lot,

On - ly what I got,
Plus a tube of grease-paint and a fol - low spot! _ I'm a
Broad - way Ba - by, ___
Slav - ing at a five and ten, _
___
Dream-ing of the great day when _ I'll be in a
no swing beat
show! ___
8va
loco

Broad-way Ba-by,
Mak-ing rounds all af-ter - noon,
Eat-ing at a greas-y spoon to save on my dough.
Solid 4
At my ti-ny flat there's just my cat, a bed and a chair.
Still I'll stick it till I'm on a bill All o - ver Times Square.

Some day, may - be,
If I stick it long e - nough,
I can get to strut my stuff,
cresc.
Work - ing for a nice man like a Zieg - feld or a Weiss - man in a great big
f
Broad - way show!

from HOW TO SUCCEED IN BUSINESS WITHOUT REALLY TRYING

Brotherhood Of Man

By Frank Loesser

C
C9
F
F#dim
B7
tie that binds
all hu - man hearts and minds
in - to one
proud to be
in that fra - ter - ni - ty,
the great big
mp
f
mf
1
C
F/C
C
D7
G7
Dm7
G7
Broth - er - hood Of Man.
Your life - long
mp
mf
2
C
Am
Dm7
G7
C
G7
Broth - er - hood Of Man?
mp
mf
f
C
G7
C
Cmaj7
Man?

from the Musical CABARET

Cabaret

Words by Fred Ebb
Music by John Kander

Bb9
1 Eb
Fm7
Bb9
2 Eb
cab - a - ret.
ret.
Come taste the
Abm
Eb
Cm
Cm+7
wine, Come hear the band, Come blow the horn, start
Cm7
F9
Bb7
Eb
cel - e - brat - ing, Right this way, your ta - ble's wait - ing.
No use per -
Start by ad -
Bb9
Bb9+5
Eb
Bb7+5
Eb
Ebmaj7
mit - ting some proph - et of doom _ To wipe ev - 'ry smile a -
mit - ting from cra - dle to tomb is - n't that long a

Bbm7
Eb7
Ab
Adim
To Coda
Gm7
C9
way;
stay;
Life is a cab - a - ret, old chum,
Fm7
Bb11
Eb
D.S. al Coda
Come to the cab - a - ret,
Come taste the
CODA
Gm7
C9
Ab
Adim
Gm7
C9
ret, old chum,
On - ly a cab - a - ret, old chum,
Fm7
Bb11
Eb
Bb9+5 Eb
so come to the cab - a - ret.
sfz
8va

from A FUNNY THING HAPPENED ON THE WAY TO THE FORUM

Comedy Tonight

Words and Music by Stephen Sondheim

G
C
F
D7
Some - thing for ev - 'ry - one, a com - e - dy to - night!
Some - thing for ev - 'ry - one, a com - e - dy to - night!
G
C
D
B
Noth - ing with kings, noth - ing with crowns.
Noth - ing of Gods, noth - ing of Fate.
F
G
Am
B
C
D11
Bring on the lov - ers, li - ars and clowns!
Weigh - ty af - fairs will just have to wait.
G
C
D
G
C
D
Old sit - u - a - tions, new com - pli - ca - tions,
Noth - ing that's for - mal, noth - ing that's nor - mal,

G
Am
G
B♭m7
Noth - ing por - ten - tous or po - lite;
No re - ci - ta - tions to re - cite!
Am7
1
D7
G
Trag - e - dy to - mor - row, com - e - dy to - night!
O - pen up the cur - tain,
Am
D
G
Am
D
2
Am7
com - e - dy
D7
G
Am
D
G
to - night!
ff
sfz

from MAN OF LA MANCHA

Dulcinea

Music by Mitch Leigh
Lyric by Joe Darion

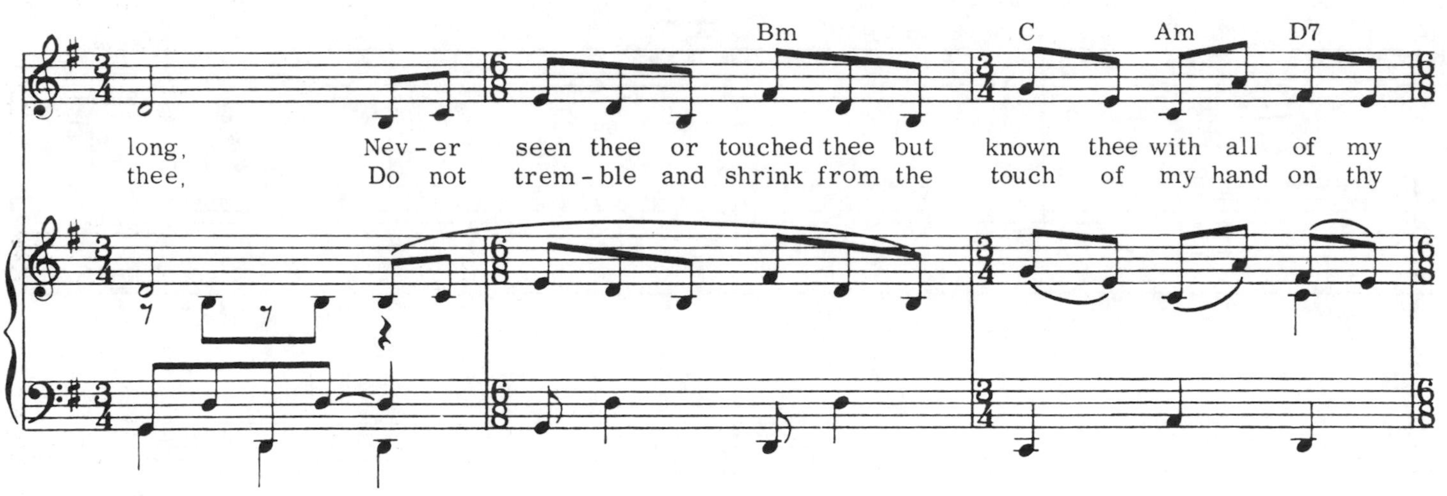

Bm
C
Am
song, Thou hast al - ways been with me, tho we have been al - ways a -
see thou art warm and a - live and no phan - tom to fade in the
D
G
G6
G
- part.
air.
Dul - ci - ne - a,
Dul - ci - ne - a,
Em
Dul - ci - ne - a,
Dul - ci - ne - a,
I see
I have
Cmaj7
C6
Cmaj7
C
D7
G6
G
heav - en when I see thee, Dul - ci - ne - a;
sought thee, sung thee, dreamed thee, Dul - ci - ne - a;

Em
And thy name is like a pray'r, an an - gel
Now I've found thee and the world shall know thy
F
Am7
rall.
whis - pers, Dul - ci - ne - a,
glo - ry, Dul - ci - ne - a,
rall.
D7
a tempo
1.
G6
G
Dul - ci - ne - a.
2. If I
Dul - ci -
a tempo
2.
G6
G
- ne - a.

from TITANIC

Godspeed Titanic (Sail On)

Music and Lyrics by Maury Yeston

Gm
Dm
berth glide free!
E♭/F
F7add4
E♭
E♭/G
F7/A
As you plow the
B♭
B♭/D
D7sus4
D7
deep, in your arms I'll
Gm
Gm/F
B♭/C
C7
keep. Safe - ly west may you car -

C
E♭/F
F7add4
F/G
G7add4
ry
me.
Sail
molto rit.
C
G/B
Am
Em
on,
sail
on,
great
ship
F
G7sus4
C
G/B
Ti
-
tan
-
ic.
Cross
the
Am
Em
o
-
pen
sea!

F/G
G7add4
F
F/A
G7/B
Pray the jour - ney's
C
C/E
E7sus4
E7
sound till your port be
Am
Am/G
Fmaj9
Dm7
found. For - tune's winds sing God -
C/G
G7sus4
F♯m7♭5
speed to thee.

C/G
For - tune's winds sing God -
G7sus4
C
C/G
speed to thee!
rit.
fff a tempo
G
N.C.
D♭/C
D/C
E♭/C
E/C
C

from MY FAIR LADY

Get Me To The Church On Time

Words by Alan Jay Lerner
Music by Frederick Loewe

Ddim
D7
B♭m6
D7/A
G
let's have a whop - per, but get me to the church on time.
G6
I got - ta be there in the morn - ing,
G
D7
spruced up and look - ing in my prime.
Girls, come and
Ddim
D7
Ddim
D7
B♭m6
D7/A
kiss me; show how you'll miss me, but get me to the church on

G
C
G
time. If I am danc - ing, roll up the floor!
A7sus
A7
D7
Am/E
F7
D9/F♯
If I am whis - tling, whewt me out the door! For
G
G6
G
I'm get - ting mar-ried in the morn - ing. Ding! Dong! The
G/F
E7
C6
Cmaj7
C+
C6
C♯dim7
bells are gon - na chime. Kick up a rum - pus, but

G/D
G+/D♯
Bm
C(add2)
G(add2)/D
don't lose the com - pass; and get me to the church, get me to the
Em7
A9
G/D
Bm
G7
A7
Am7/D
D7
church, for Pete's sake, get me to the church on
G
1
D7
2
time!
f

from THE KING AND I

Getting To Know You

Lyrics by Oscar Hammerstein II
Music by Richard Rodgers

F♯dim7
C/G
A7
Am7
learn - ing (You'll for - give me if I boast.) And I've now be - come an
D7
Dm7/G
G7
(Spoken)
ex - pert On the sub - ject I like most, Get - ting to know you.
Refrain (gracefully and not fast)
C
Dm7
G7
Get - ting to know you, get - ting to know all a - bout you
mp
tranquillo
Dm7
G7
C
Get - ting to like you, get - ting to hope you like me

Fmaj7
F6
Get - ting to know you, Put - ting it my way, but nice - ly
F+
F
Am7
D7
Dm7/G
You are pre - cise - ly My cup of tea!
cresc.
mf
G7
C
Dm7
G7
Get - ting to know you, get - ting to feel free and eas - y
f
p
Dm7
G7
Dm7
G7
Dm7
G7
C7
When I am with you, get - ting to know what to say.

Fmaj7 F6 Dm7 G7
Have-n't you no - ticed? Sud - den - ly I'm bright and
Cmaj7 C7 F C Dm7 G7
breez - y Be - cause of all the beau - ti - ful and new
poco a poco cresc.
C(add9) Am7 D7 Am7 D7 Dm7 G7
things I'm learn-ing a - bout you day by
1 C G7
day. Get-ting to
f p
2 C F C
day.
mf

from Meredith Willson's THE MUSIC MAN

Goodnight, My Someone

By Meredith Willson

G
C
G7
night.
Sweet dreams be yours dear if dreams there
C
D♯dim
C
G7
be; Sweet dreams to car - ry you close to me. I
C
C7
F
D7
D♯dim
C
wish they may and I wish they might. Now good - night, My
G
1
C
C♯dim
G7
2
C
Fm6
C
Some - one, Good - night. Good - night.

from HELLO, DOLLY!

Hello, Dolly!

Music and Lyric by Jerry Herman

Bb6 Bb Bbdim F7 Bb Gm
go - in' strong. We feel the room sway - in', for the band's
Fm7 Bb7 Fm7 Bb7 Ebmaj7 Eb6 Cm6 D7
play - in' one of your old fa - v'rite songs from 'way back when. So
Gm Dm Gm Dm C9 C9+5
take her wrap, fel - las, Find her an emp - ty lap, fel - las,
gol - ly gee, fel - las, Find her a va - cant knee, fel - las,
Dol - ly 'll nev - er
Cm7 F9 Bb Bdim Cm7 F7 Cm7 F9 C9 C9+5
go a - way a - gain! Hel - go a - way, Dol-ly 'll nev - er
Cm7 F9 C9 C9+5 Cm7 F9 Bb F7 Bb
go a - way, Dol-ly 'll nev - er go a - way a - gain!

from THE KING AND I

Hello, Young Lovers

Lyrics by Oscar Hammerstein II
Music by Richard Rodgers

A
D/F♯
Fdim7
will. There are new lov - ers now on the
mf
mp
A7/E
E♭7♭5
D
Dm6
same si - lent hill, Look - ing on the same blue sea. And I
A
Dm
know Tom and I are a part of them all, And they're all a part of Tom
Gracefully
G7
C
C6
Cmaj7
C6
and me. Hel -
rit.
mf a tempo

Refrain (very moderately)
C(add9) C Cmaj7 C6
lo, young lov - ers, who - ev - er you are, I
Cmaj7 C6 G7/B Fm/C
hope your trou - bles are few
All my good
G7/B E♭/B♭ 6fr G7/B Dm7 Dm7/G G7
wish - es go with you to - night —
I've been in love like
C C(add9) C Cmaj7
you.
Be brave, young lov - ers, and fol - low your
p
mf
p

C6
Cmaj7
C6
G7/B
star, Be brave and faith - ful and true.
Fm/C
G7/B
E♭/B♭
6fr
G7/B
Dm7
Cling ver - y close to each oth - er to - night —
I've been in
Dm7/G
G7
C
F/A
C7sus/G
3fr
love like you.
I know how it feels to have
mf
mp
F/A
C7sus/G
3fr
F/A
C7sus/G
3fr
C7
F
wings on your heels, And to fly down a street in a trance.

E7
Am
You fly down a street on a chance that you'll meet, And you
Dm7
Dm7/G
G7
meet — not real - ly by chance.
Don't
p
C(add9)
C
Cmaj7
C6
Cmaj7
cry, young lov - ers, What - ev - er you do, Don't cry be -
C6
G7/B
Fm/C
G7/B
cause I'm a - lone.
All of my mem - 'ries are

E♭/B♭
6fr
G7/B
Dm7
G7
hap - py to - night—
I've had a love of my
C7
F/A
Fm/A♭
own,
I've had a love of my
mf
C+/G
C6/G
Dm
E♭/G
3fr
G7
own, like yours,
I've had a love of my
cresc. ed allargando
1
C6
G7
2
C6
own.
Hel -
own.
mf a tempo
p
f

from FINIAN'S RAINBOW

How Are Things In Glocca Morra

Words by E.Y. Harburg
Music by Burton Lane

C13
Gm7
C13
G♭dim
Gm7
Edim
F7
G7
D♭dim
C7
breeze; it well may be it's fol - lowed me a - cross the
F
B♭
F
C7♭9
F
B♭
F
Gm7/C
seas. Then tell me, please: please: how are things in Gloc - ca
B♭/F
Fmaj7
Gm7
Fmaj7
Gm7
C7
Gm7
Mor - ra? Is that lit - tle brook still leap - ing there?
C7
Gm7
C13
Gm7
C13
Does it still run down to Don - ny cove? Through Kil - ly - begs, Kil -

F
B♭
F/A
B♭
F/A
Gm7/C
B♭/F
Fmaj7
Gm7
3fr
ker - ry and Kil - dare?
How are things in Gloc - ca Mor - ra?
Fmaj7
Gm7
C7
Gm7
C7
Is that wil - low tree still weep - ing there?
Does that lad - die lass - ie with the
Gm7
C13
2fr
C7
twin - klin' eye come whis - tlin' smil - in' by and does he she walk a - way, sad and
Gm7
C7
F
C7/F
F
A7
dream - y there not to see me there?
So I

B♭ C7 F A7 B♭ C7 F A7
ask each weep - in' wil - low and each brook a - long the way, and each
B♭ Gm7 C7 Fmaj7 D7♭9
lad that comes a - whis - tlin' too - ra - lay, "How are
lass a - sigh - in'
Gm Am Gm7/C C7 F
things in Gloc - ca Mor - ra this fine day?
Gm7/C F
How are things in Gloc - ca day?"

from HOW TO SUCCEED IN BUSINESS WITHOUT REALLY TRYING

I Believe In You

By Frank Loesser

G D G Cmaj7 Db7 D7 G
You, I Be - lieve In You.
R.H.
G#dim G Eb7 Ab Bbm7 Eb7-5 Ab
I hear the And when my faith in my fel - low man
Bbm7 Db9 Cm7 F7 Bb Cm7 F7
all but falls a - part, I've but to feel your hand
Bb Gm7 C7 D7sus D7 G#dim
grasp - ing mine and I take heart, I take heart. To see the
rit.

Am7
D9
C
C#m7
F#7
Bm
C
cool clear eyes of a seek-er of wis-dom and truth,
Bm
G#dim
Am7
D9
C
C#m7
F#7
Yet there's that slam bang tang rem - i - nis-cent of gin and ver -
B
C
B
Cmaj7
Db7
D7
G
mouth.
Oh I Be - lieve In You,
Cmaj7
Db7
D7
Cmaj7
D11
Gmaj7
I Be - lieve In You.
R.H.

from HAIRSPRAY

I Can Hear The Bells

Music by Marc Shaiman
Lyrics by Marc Shaiman and Scott Wittman

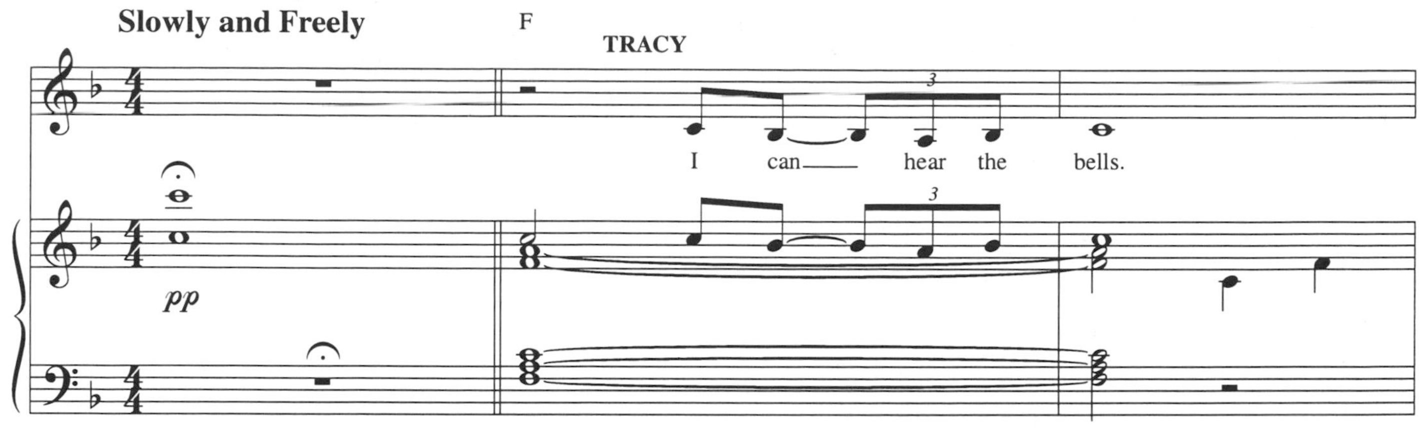

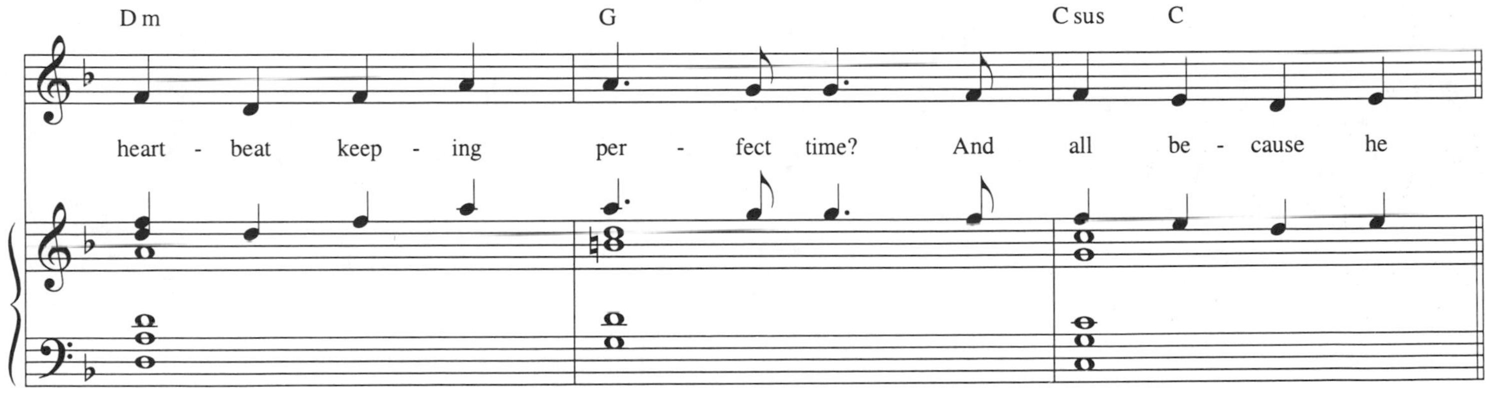

B♭
F/A
heart was_ un-pre-pared when he tapped me and knocked me off my feet.
G 7sus
G 7
B♭maj9/C
F
One lit - tle touch, now my life's com - plete. 'Cause when he nudged me, love
mp
D m
put me_ in a fix. Yes, it hit me just like a_ ton of bricks. Yes, my
B♭
F/A
F/G
G 7
heart burst. Now I know what_life's a-bout. One lit - tle touch and love's

F/C Csus C F F/E
knocked me out, and I can hear the bells. My head is spin - ning.
mf
Dm Dm/C B♭
I can hear the bells. Some - thing's be - gin - ning. Ev - 'ry - bod - y says that a
F/A F/G G7 Dm/C C B♭/C C
girl who looks like me can't win his love. Well, just wait and see, 'cause
F F/E Dm
I can hear the bells. Just hear them chim - ing. I can hear the bells. My
mf

Dm/C
B♭
F/A
temp - 'ra - ture's climb - ing. I can't con - tain my joy 'cause I fin - 'ly found the boy I've been
F/G
G7
C7sus
F
miss - in'. Lis - ten! I can hear the be - ells.
(ding!)
mp
B♭/C
F
D♭sus
D♭
G♭
G♭/F
E♭m
Round one, he'll ask me on a date, and then round two, I'll
f
mf

C♭
G♭/B♭
primp, but won't be late be - cause round three's when we kiss in - side his car. Won't
G♭/A♭
A♭7
G♭/D♭
D♭
D♭sus2
D♭
G♭
go all the way, but I'll go pret - ty far. Then round four, he'll
mf
G♭/F
E♭m
ask me for my hand, and then round five, we'll book the wed - ding band, so by
C♭
G♭/B♭
G♭/A♭
A♭7
round six, Am - ber, much to your sur - prise, this heav - y - weight cham - pi - on

Ebm/Db Db Cb/Db Db
Gb
Gb/F
takes the prize and
I can— hear the bells.
My ears are ring - ing.
f
Ebm
Ebm/Db Cb
I can— hear the bells. The
brides - maids are sing - ing.
Ev - 'ry - bod - y says that a
mf
Gb/Bb
Ab7sus Ab7
Ebm/Db Db Cb/Db Db
guy who's such a gem
won't look my way. Well, the
laugh's on them 'cause
Gb
Gb/F Ebm
I can— hear the bells. My
fa - ther will smile...——
I can— hear the bells. ...as he
f

E♭m/D♭
C♭
G♭/B♭
walks me down the aisle. My moth-er starts to cry, but I can't see 'cause Link and I are French-
mf
G♭/A♭
A♭7
D♭7sus
G♭
kiss - in'. Lis - ten! I can hear the bells.
(ding!)
mp
C♭/G♭
G♭
D sus
D
G
G/F♯
Em
I can hear the bells. My head is reel - in'. I can hear the bells. I
ff

Em/D
C
G/B
can't stop the peal - in'. Ev - 'ry - bod - y warns that he won't like what he'll see, but
f
G/A
A7
Em/D
D
C/D
D
G
I know that he'll look in - side of me. Yeah, I can hear the bells. To -
ff
G/F♯
Em
Em/D
day's just the start 'cause I can hear the bells, and 'til death do us part. And
C
G/B
Am7
e - ven when we die we'll look down from up a - bove, re - mem - ber - ing the night that we
mp

G/B
G7/B
C
two fell in love. We both will share a tear, and he'll
G/B
G/A
A
D7sus
whis - per as we're rem - i - ni - scin'. Lis - ten! I can hear the
colla voce
(ding!)
G
G7/F
Em7
bells. I can hear the bells.
ritard
C m/E♭
G
I can hear the bells.

from PAL JOEY

I Could Write A Book

Words by Lorenz Hart
Music by Richard Rodgers

Gm7
3fr
C7
Fmaj7
Em7
A7
But my bus - y mind is burn-ing to use what learn-ing I've got.
D7
G/D
G7
Dm7
G7
I won't waste an - y time; I'll strike while the i - ron is hot. If they
C
G7
C
G7
asked me, I could write a book a - bout the
C
G7
C6
C♯dim7
Dm7
G7
G7/F
way you walk and whis - per and look. I could

C/E
A♭7/E♭
Dm7
G7
C
Cdim7
write a pre - face on how we
G/B
C
Cdim7
G/B
E♭7/B♭
Am7
D7
met so the world would nev - er for -
G
Dm7
G7
C
get. And the sim - ple
G7
C
G7
se - cret of the plot is just to

C G7 C6 C♯dim7 Dm7
tell them that I love you a lot.
G7 G7/F C/E A♭7/E♭ Dm7 G7
Then the world dis - cov - ers, as
Gm7 C7 F Dm7 C/G C+/E F6 G7
3fr
my book ends, how to make two lov - ers of
1 C Dm7 G7
friends. If they
2 C F F/C C
friends.

from TITANIC

I Must Get On That Ship

Music and Lyrics by Maury Yeston

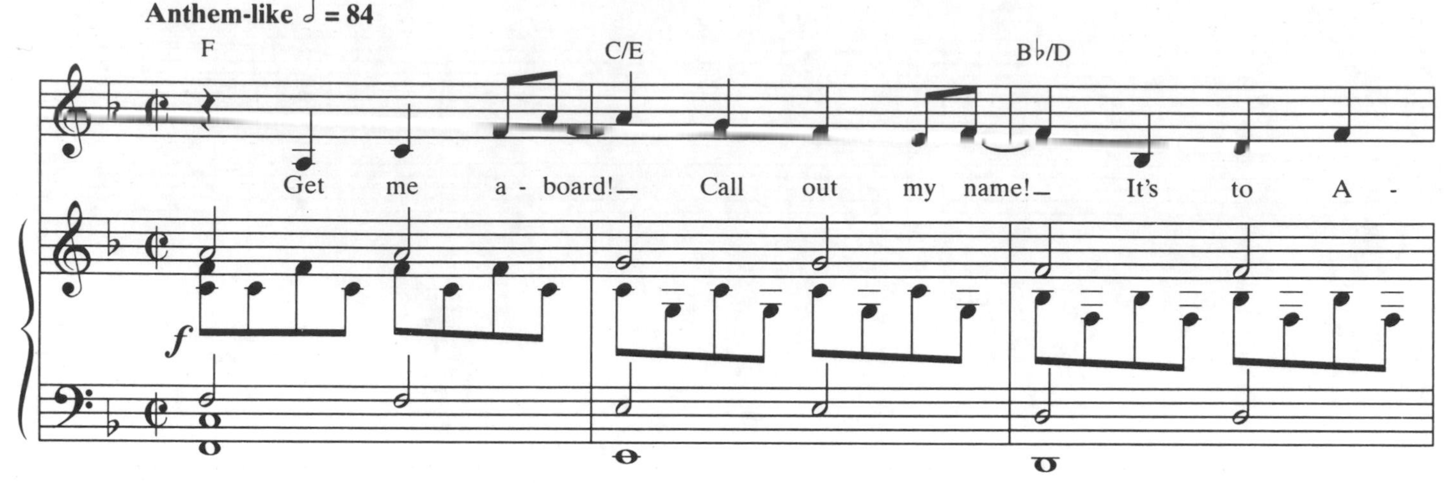

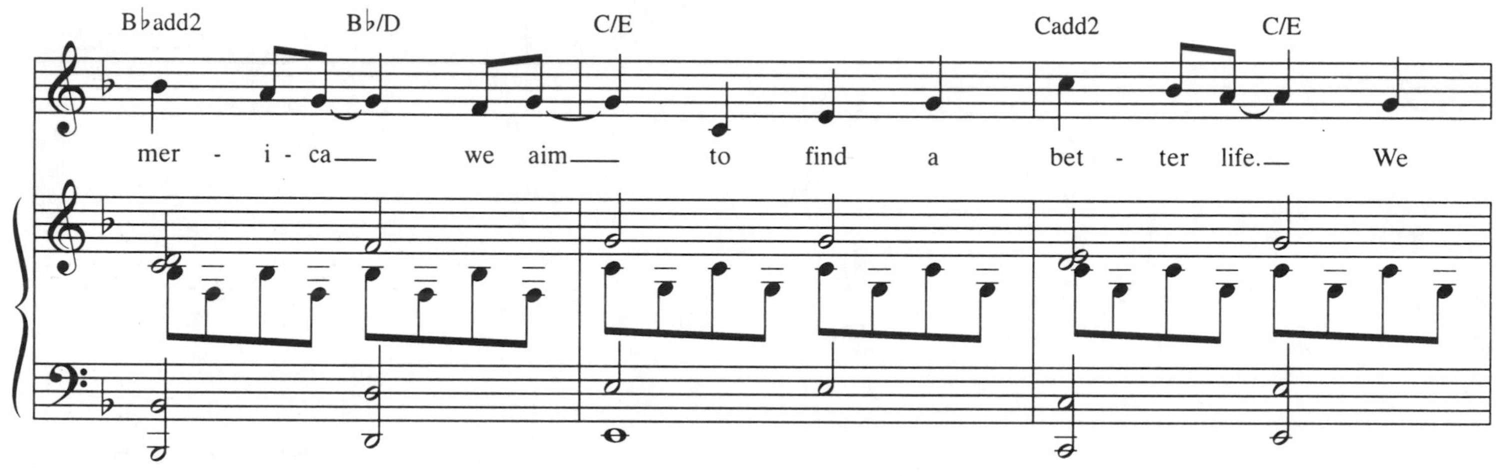

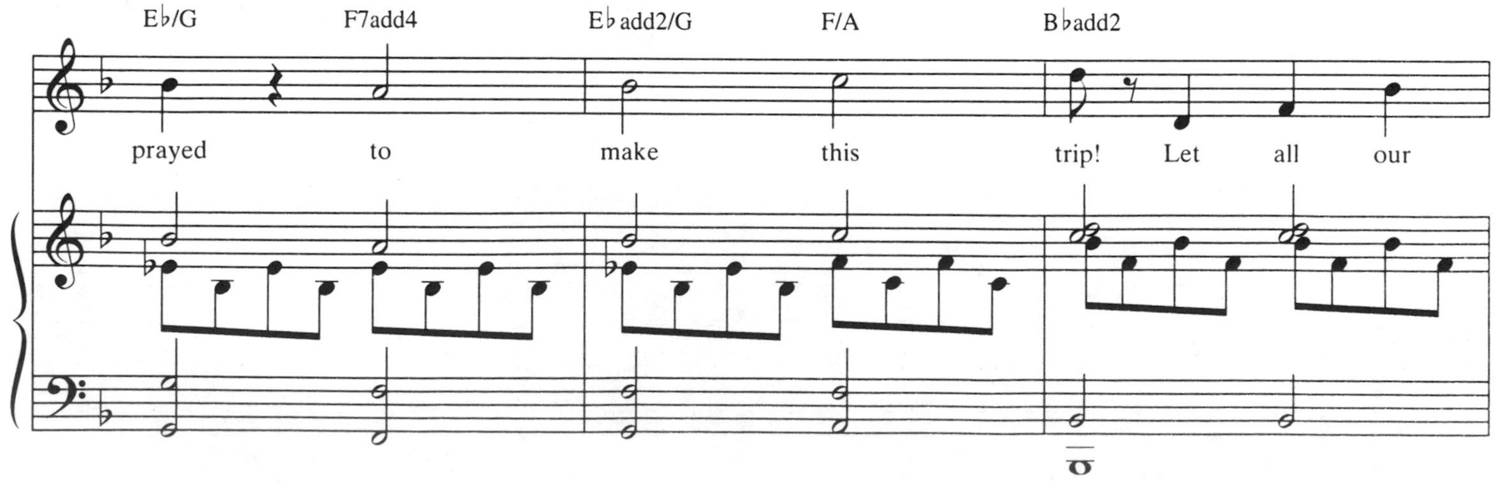

B♭/D
E♭add2
E♭add2/G
chil - dren's chil - dren know that this day long a - go we
B♭/F
F7sus4
F7
B♭
dreamt of them and came a - board this ship!
F/A
B♭
Gm7
F
B♭
F7/C
B♭/D
B♭
For the maid - en voy - age! For the maid - en
ff
Fadd2
Gm
D7sus4
voy - age! Get us all a - board!

A little faster 𝅗𝅥 = 88

N.C. G D/F♯

Can't wait to board that ship to - day,

C/E Cadd2 C/E D/F♯

be with her when she pulls a - way and takes her

gliss. R.H.

Dadd2 D/F♯ F/A G7sus4 Fadd2/A G/B

maid - en sail. I must get on that

Cadd2 C/E Fadd2

ship. The larg - est, grand - est on the earth, and I've re -

Am7
C/G
G7sus4
G7
served a berth to be a - board. Now point me toward that
C
Am7
G
ship! The fin - est
D/F♯
C/E
Cadd2
C/E
peo - ple will at - tend; the best a - mong them we'll be - friend.
D/F♯
D
D/F♯
F/A
G7sus4
They'll stand right next to us, be at my

Fadd2/A
G/B
Cadd2
C/E
fin - ger - tip! Great heads of state and mil - lion - aires
Fadd2
Fadd2/A
C/G
who run the world's af - fairs will all be there. I
G7sus4
G7
C
G/B
C
Am7
must get on that ship! For the maid - en
G
C
G7/D
C/E
C
G/B
Am
voy - age! For the maid - en voy - age!

D7sus4
Get us all a - board.
rit.
Tempo I (𝅗𝅥 = 84)
Broadly, and with nobility
G
D/F♯
C/E
Lift up the ramp, let go the lines, raise up her
f
C
C/E
D/F♯
D
D/F♯
col - ors and de - signs! Pre - pare for cast - ing off, and
F/A
G7sus4
F/A
G/B
C
through the port we'll slip! Each per - son

C/E
Fadd2
F/A
stand - ing at the rail, let one great thought pre - vail, one
C/G
sin - gle prayer...
God
G7sus4
G9sus4
bless this no -
G7sus4
C
ble ship!

from GRAND HOTEL

I Want To Go To Hollywood

Words and Music by Maury Yeston

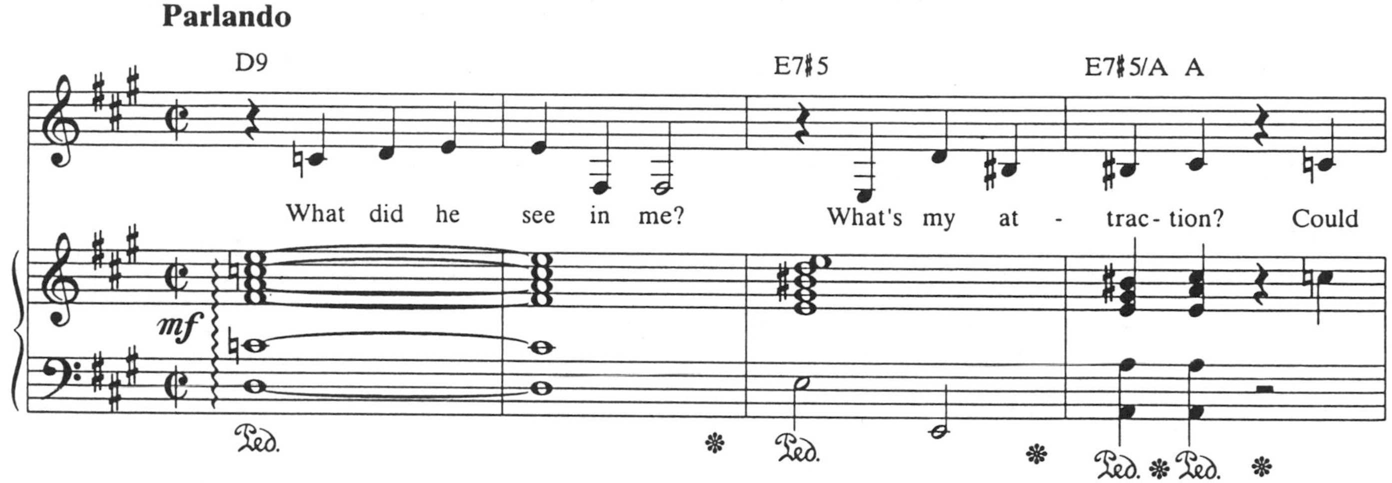

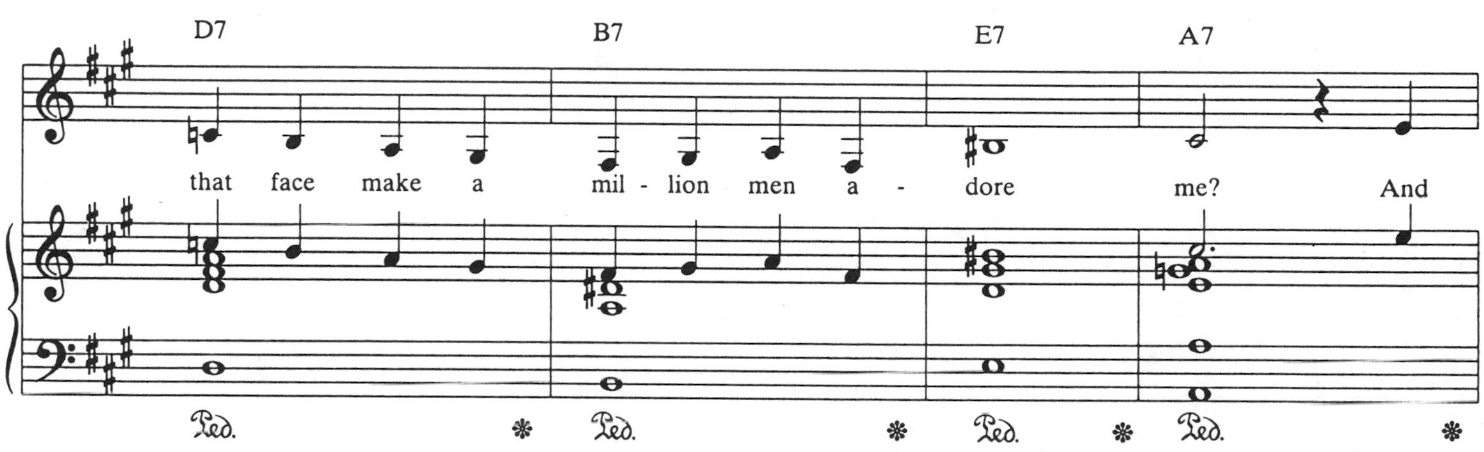

B7
B7/D♯
E7♯5
E13
that the girl I see there right be - fore me?
With a swing 𝅗𝅥 = 92
A
E+
Em/A
mf
I wan - na be that girl in the mir - ror there. I wan - na be that
girl with gold - en hair. Up on a sil - ver screen, most ev - 'ry - where

F♯7 Eadd2/G♯ F♯7/A♯ F♯7 Eadd2/G♯ F♯7/A♯ B7add4
in the world. I want to
E7sus4 E7 Aadd2 B7♯5 E9♭5
go to Hol-ly-wood! Talk-ies! I mean the pic-tures.
A E+ Em/A E+ A E+
I wan-na have a hot time ev-'ry night, get out and raise a lit-
Em/A E+ A E+ Em/A E+
tle Fahr-en-heit, knock ev-'ry Duke and Count and Bar-on right

F♯7 Eadd2/G♯ F♯7/A♯ F♯7 Eadd2/G♯ F♯7/A♯ B7add4 E7sus4 E7
off his feet! I'll be that girl that's un-der-
C♯7♯5 Em/F♯ F♯7 B7add4 E7sus4 E7
stood! Oh! I want to go to Hol-ly-
A9 G/B Cm A7/C♯ Cm G/B A9 D9
wood. I wan-na sing the blues. I wan-na wear nice
sim.
A9 B7
shoes and drink il-le-gal booze in ev-'ry

G7
E9♯5
A
E+
late - night spot for "Le Jazz Hot."
I wan - na break - fast,
Em/A
E+
A
E+
Em/A
E+
lunch and din - ner there,
if I'm a big box
of - fice win - ner there.
A
E+
Em/A
E+
F♯7
Eadd2/G♯
I'll be the most well - known Ber - lin - er there ev - er was!
F♯7/A♯
F♯7
Eadd2/G♯
F♯7/A♯
B7add4
E7sus4
E7
A add2
G♯+
Em/G
I want to go to Hol - ly - wood,

F♯7 F♯7/A♯ B7add4 E7sus4 E7 B♭(♭5)/A
so I can get far a - way from:
B♭(♭5)/A
Fried - rich - stras - se. My cold
A♭m7♭5
wa - ter flat. The so - fa that I sleep on be - hind the
mp
sim.
Bm7♭5
screen. The nois - y lodg - er in the next room.

A♭m7♭5
My bro - ken hand mir - ror. My bro - ken cof - fee pot.
Bm7♭5
If things get bro - ken, they stay bro - ken in
B♭(♭5)/A
Fried - rich - stras - se.
A♭m7♭5
The worn - out bris - tles on your
mf
p subito
hair - brush.
Bm7♭5
The pen - nies need - ed for the heat ev - 'ry

A♭m7♭5
hour. And when you get sick, you stay sick in
B♭(♭5)/A
Dadd2/E
Fried - rich - stras - se. Where you live with lit - tle soap and with
hard - ly an - y hope.
A E+ Em/A E+
A E+ Em/A E+ A E+
I wan - na be that

Em/A E+ A E+ Em/A E+
girl in the mir - ror there. I wan - na be that girl with gold - en hair,
A E+ Em/A E+ F♯7 Eadd2/G♯
up on a sil - ver screen, most ev - 'ry - where in the world.
F♯7/A♯ F♯7 Eadd2/G♯ F♯7/A♯ B7add4 E7sus4 E7 B7
I want to go to Hol - ly-, I want to go, I want
E7sus4 E7 Aadd2 G♯+ Em/G F♯7 F♯7/A♯ B7
to go, I want to go, I want to go, I want to go, I have to go, I have

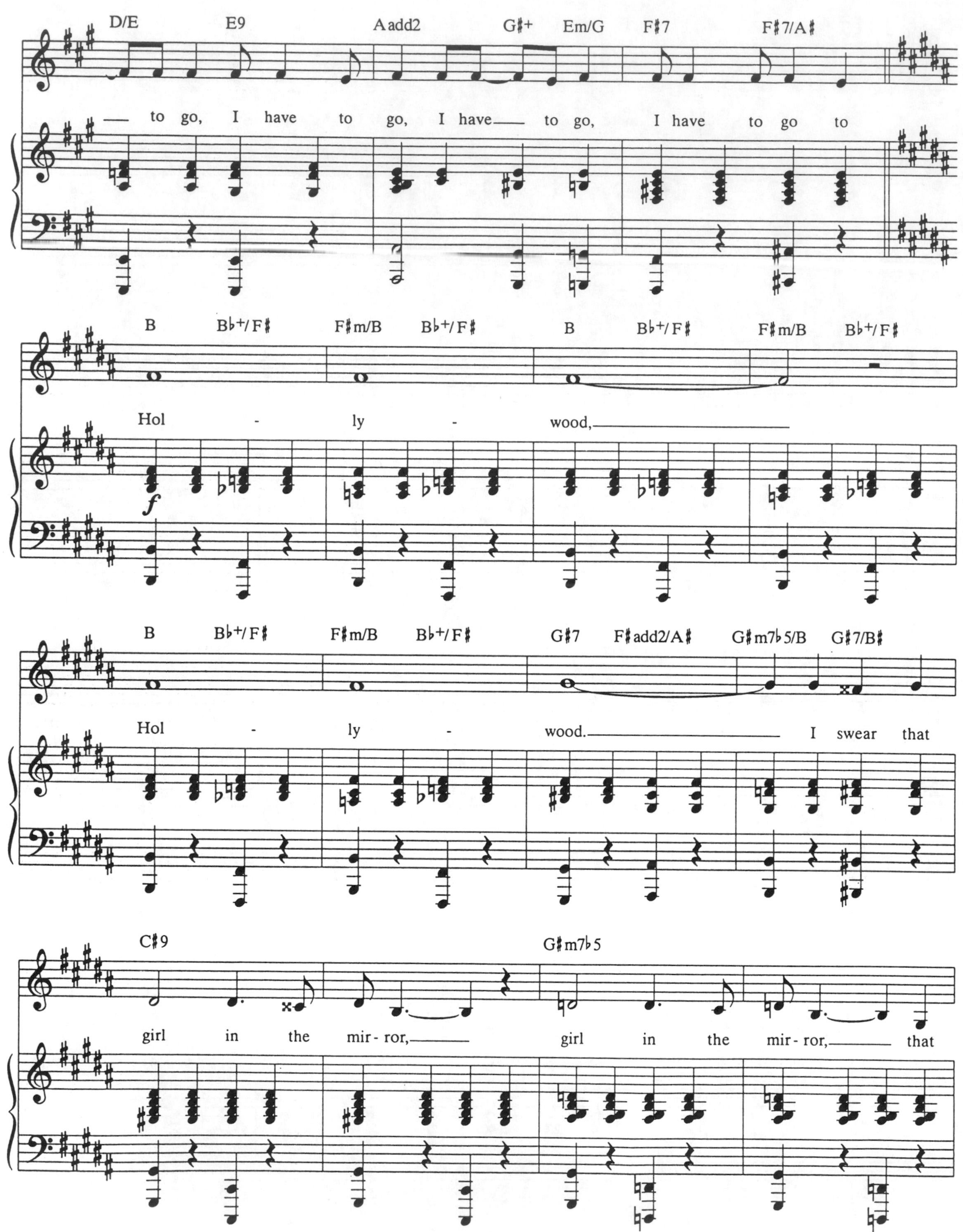
D/E E9 Aadd2 G♯+ Em/G F♯7 F♯7/A♯
— to go, I have to go, I have — to go, I have to go to
B B♭+/F♯ F♯m/B B♭+/F♯ B B♭+/F♯ F♯m/B B♭+/F♯
Hol - ly - wood, —
f
B B♭+/F♯ F♯m/B B♭+/F♯ G♯7 F♯add2/A♯ G♯m7♭5/B G♯7/B♯
Hol - ly - wood. — I swear that
C♯9 G♯m7♭5
girl in the mir - ror, — girl in the mir - ror, — that

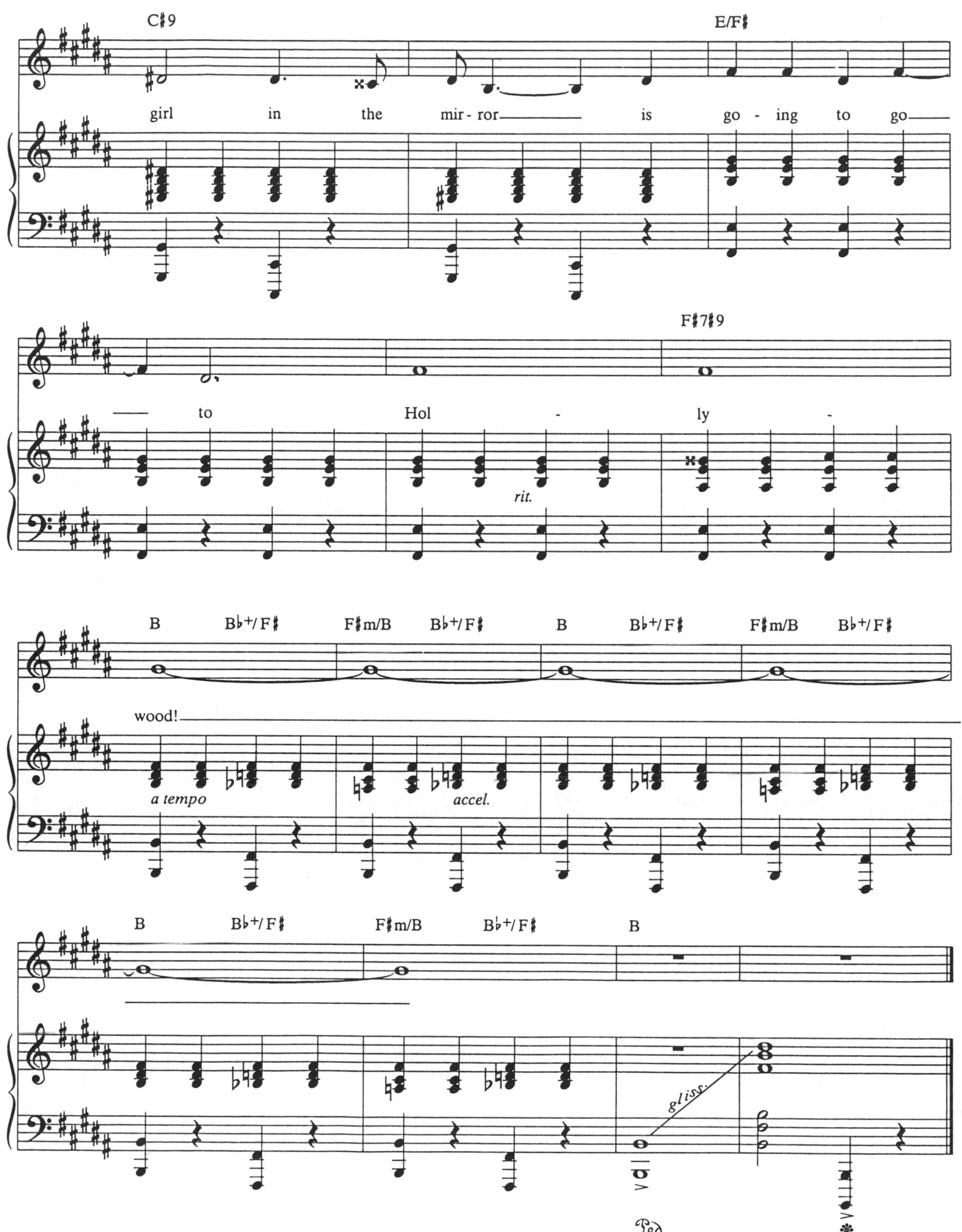
C♯9
E/F♯
girl in the mir - ror is go - ing to go
to Hol - ly -
F♯7♯9
rit.
B Bb+/F♯ F♯m/B Bb+/F♯ B Bb+/F♯ F♯m/B Bb+/F♯
wood!
a tempo
accel.
B Bb+/F♯ F♯m/B Bb+/F♯ B
gliss.
Ped.
*

from CAMELOT

If Ever I Would Leave You

Words by Alan Jay Lerner
Music by Frederick Loewe

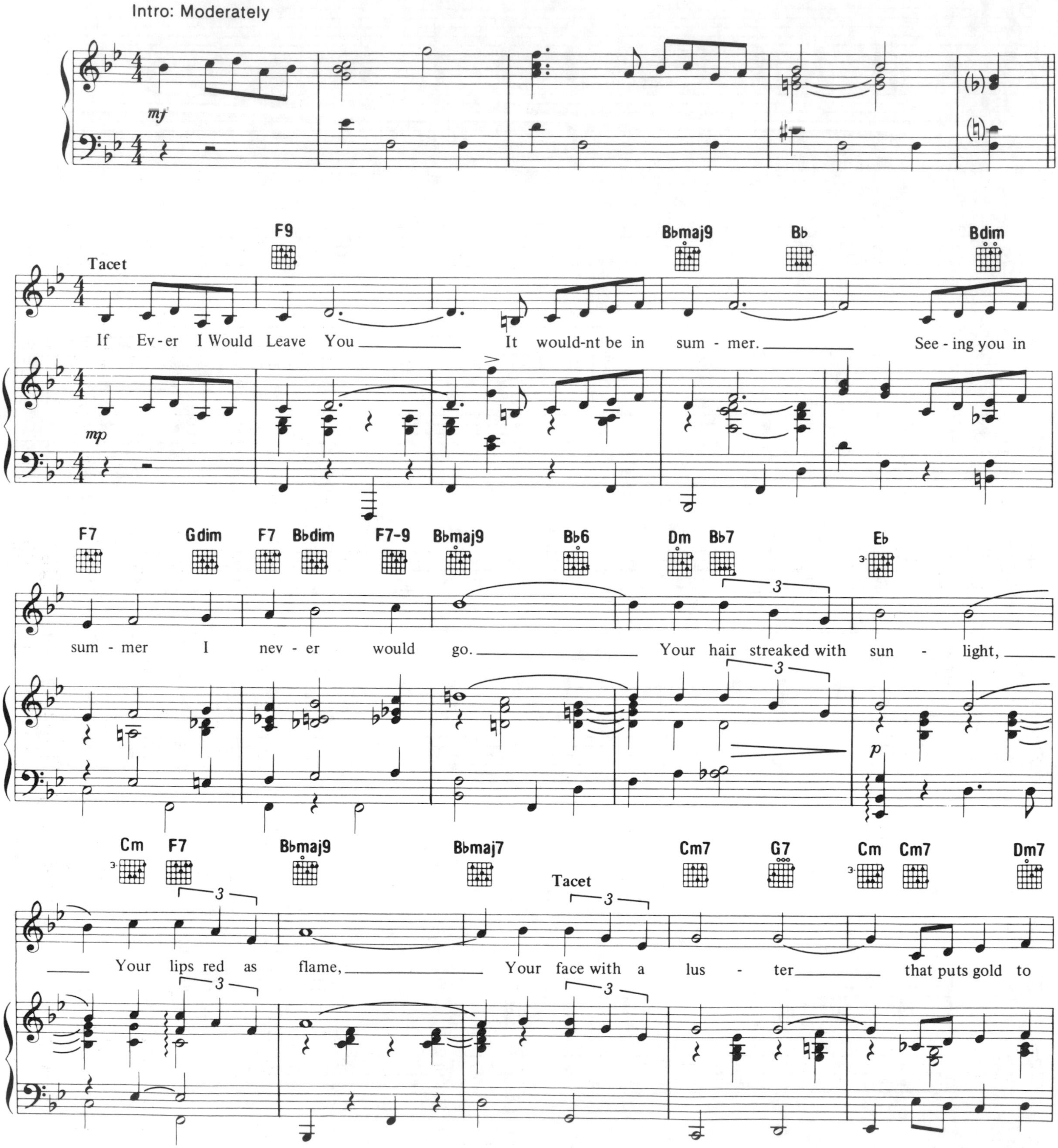

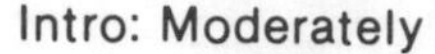

Intro: Moderately
mf
Tacet
F9
Bbmaj9
Bb
Bdim
mp
If Ev-er I Would Leave You It would-nt be in sum-mer. See-ing you in
F7
Gdim
F7
Bbdim
F7-9
Bbmaj9
Bb6
Dm
Bb7
Eb
sum-mer I nev-er would go. Your hair streaked with sun-light,
p
Cm
F7
Bbmaj9
Bbmaj7
Tacet
Cm7
G7
Cm
Cm7
Dm7
Your lips red as flame, Your face with a lus-ter that puts gold to

Cm7 F7 F9 Bbmaj9 Bb6
Tacet
shame! But if I'd ev-er leave you, It could-n't be in au-tumn.
Bbmaj9 Bdim F7 Gdim F7 Bbdim F7-9 Bbmaj9 Bb6 Dm Bb7
How I'd leave in au-tumn I nev-er will know. I've seen how you
Eb Cm F7 Bbmaj9 Bbmaj7 Cm7 G7
Tacet
spar-kle When fall nips the air. I know you in au-tumn
Cm Cm7 F7-9 Bb Ebm Bb D D+ D6 G A7
And I must be there. And could I leave you run-ning mer-ri-ly through the
R.H.
D Dmaj7 D6 F# B F# Em7 A7
snow? Or on a win-try eve-ning when you catch the fi-re's

D
F7
F9
glow? If Ev - er I Would Leave You, How could it be in
Bbmaj9
Fdim
Cm7
F
Gdim
F7
spring - time, Know - ing how in spring I'm be - witched by you
D7sus
D7
Gm7
Dm
Bb7
Eb
Ebmaj7
Cm7
Ebm
so? Oh, no! not in spring - time! Sum - mer, win - ter or
Bb
C9
F9
Cm7
F7-9
fall! No, nev - er could I leave you at
pp subito
Bb6
Bb6
B6
Bb
all! And could I all!
8va
cresc.

from JEKYLL & HYDE

In His Eyes

Words by Leslie Bricusse
Music by Frank Wildhorn

E♭
B♭/F
F7
B♭/F
F7sus4
F7
think of him, then I re - mem - ber, re - mem - ber...
Moderately, with a beat
B♭add2
Cm7/B♭
Cm7♭5/B♭
B♭add2
E♭/B♭
In his eyes, I can see where my heart
mf
F/A
B♭add2
Gm
Gm/F
E♭add2
Cm7♭5
longs to be! In his eyes, I see a gen - tle glow; and
B♭add2
Cm7/B♭
Cm7♭5/B♭
Gm
that's where I'll be safe, I know!

Em7♭5
E♭maj7
F/A
B♭add2
Safe in his arms, close to his heart;
Gm
E♭maj7
Fsus4
E♭/F
but I don't know quite where to start. By look - ing
rit.
F/B♭
B♭add2
F/G
Gm
E♭maj7
in his eyes, will I see be - yond to - mor - row?
If I'm wise, I will walk a - way and glad - ly.
a tempo
Fsus4 sus2
F/B♭
B♭add2
F/G
Gm
By look - ing in his eyes, will I see be - yond the
But sad - ly, I'm not wise. It's hard to talk a - way the

E♭maj7
Fsus4
F
E♭
Dm7
sor - row that I feel? Will his eyes re - veal to me
mem - 'ries that you prize! Love is worth for - giv - ing for!
mf
E♭
B♭add2/D
E♭
Dm7
To Coda
prom - is - es or lies? But he can't con - ceal from me the
Now I re - al - ize. Ev - 'ry - thing worth liv - ing for is
Cm7
Cm7♭5/F
F7
Gm7♭5
G♭maj7
love in his eyes! His eyes! His
I know their ev - 'ry look. They're like an o - pen book.
D.S. al Coda
C7♭9
E♭/F
F7
E♭/F
Cm7/F
eyes! But most of all the look that hyp - no - tized me!
rit. e cresc.

Coda
Cm7 Eb/F F Gm7 C7sus4 C7
there, in his eyes!
cresc.
ff
Eb Dm7 Eb Bbadd2/D
Love is worth for - giv - ing for! Now I re - al - ize.
Eb Dm7 Cm7 Eb/F F Eb Dm7
Ev - 'ry - thing worth liv - ing for is there, in his eyes!
rit.
a tempo
Eb Bbadd2/D Eb Eb/F B
rit.
mp

from CAROUSEL

If I Loved You

Lyrics by Oscar Hammerstein II
Music by Richard Rodgers

Allegretto moderato

N.C.

mp

A7 D

p

When I worked in the mill, Weav-in' at the loom, I'd gaze ab-sent-
Kind-a scraw-ny and pale, Pick-in' at my food And love-sick like

Db

mind-ed at the roof And half the time the shut-tle 'd
an-y oth-er guy I'd throw a-way my sweat-er and

tan-gle in the threads, And the warp 'd get mixed with the woof
dress up like a dude in a dick-ey and a col-lar and a tie

A
If I loved you!
If I loved you!
Oh,
Oh,
D/F♯
C(add9)/G
C/G
G7
some - how I can see just ex - ack - ly how I'd be.
p
rit.
Refrain (with great warmth and slowly)
C
Cdim7
C/E
E+
If I loved you,
Time and a - gain I would try to say
mf
Dm/F
D♯dim7
C/E
Em
All I'd want you to know.
cross hands

C
Cdim7
C/E
If I loved you, Words wouldn't come in an
E+
Dm/F
D♯dim7
C/E
eas - y way, 'Round in cir - cles I'd go.
cresc.
E+
Am
Dm
C♯7
Long - in' to tell you, but a - fraid and
mf espr.
C/G
Dm/F
B♭
D/A
shy, I'd let my gold - en chanc - es pass me

G
G7
C
Cdim7
C/E
by! Soon you'd leave me, off you would go in the
E+
Dm/F
D♯dim7
C/G
Em
mist of day, Nev - er, nev - er to know
C
Em
Dm/F
C/E
Dm7
Dm7/G
G7
How I loved you, If I
mf molto espr.
f
rit.
C
Dm7/G
G7
C
loved you.
loved you.
a tempo
L.H.

from MAN OF LA MANCHA

The Impossible Dream (The Quest)

Lyric by Joe Darion
Music by Mitch Leigh

1
Bbm
Eb7
run where the brave dare not go. 2. To
2
Bbm
Eb7
Bbm7
reach the un - reach - a - ble star! This is my
Ab
Fm
quest, to fol - low that star, No mat - ter how
Cm
Db6
hope - less, no mat - ter how far; To fight for the

Fm
E
E+
right without - out ques - tion or
pause. To be will - ing to
Ab/Eb
Ab+5/E
Fm
Gb
march in - to hell for a heav - en - ly
cause! And I
Bbm
Gb
know, if I'll on - ly be
true To this glo - ri - ous
C
Db6
quest, that my
heart will lie peace - ful and

G7#9
Db m
(Tacet)
Ab maj9
calm, When I'm laid to my rest, And the world will be bet-ter for
mf
Db maj9
this; That one man, scorned and cov - ered with
Cm
Cm7
Db 6
scars, Still strove with his last ounce of cour-age, To
Ab
rall.
Eb9
Bbm7/Eb
a tempo
Ab
reach the un-reach-a-ble stars.
rall.
a tempo
fz
fz

from GYPSY

Let Me Entertain You

Words by Stephen Sondheim
Music by Jule Styne

F
Fm
C/E
Cdim/E♭
4fr
Dm7
D7
3
And if you're real good,
I'll make you feel good;
I want your spir - its to
G7
C
A9
G/B
Cm6
A7/C♯
climb.
Just
let
me
en - ter - tain
you,
and
Dm
A7/E
Dm/F
G7
C7
E7
A7
Dm
Edim7
we'll have a real good
time, yes sir,
we'll
have
a
Dm/F
G7
1
C
E♭dim7
Dm7
G7
2
C
real
good
time.
time.

from VICTOR/VICTORIA

Living In The Shadows

Words by Leslie Bricusse
Music by Frank Wildhorn

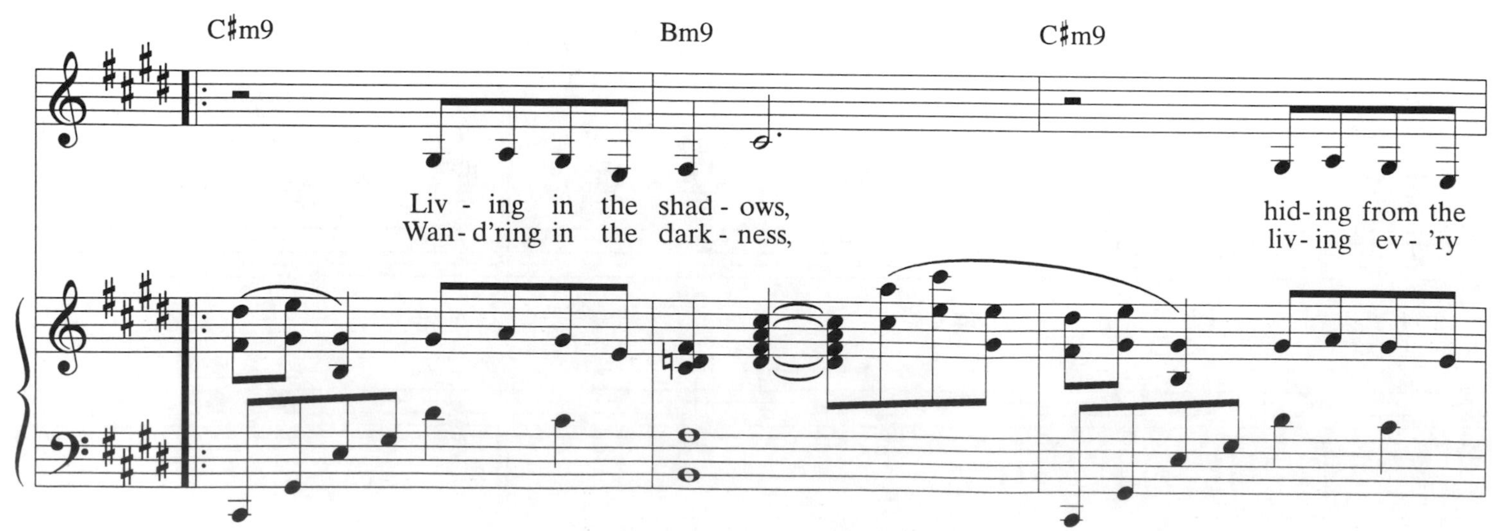

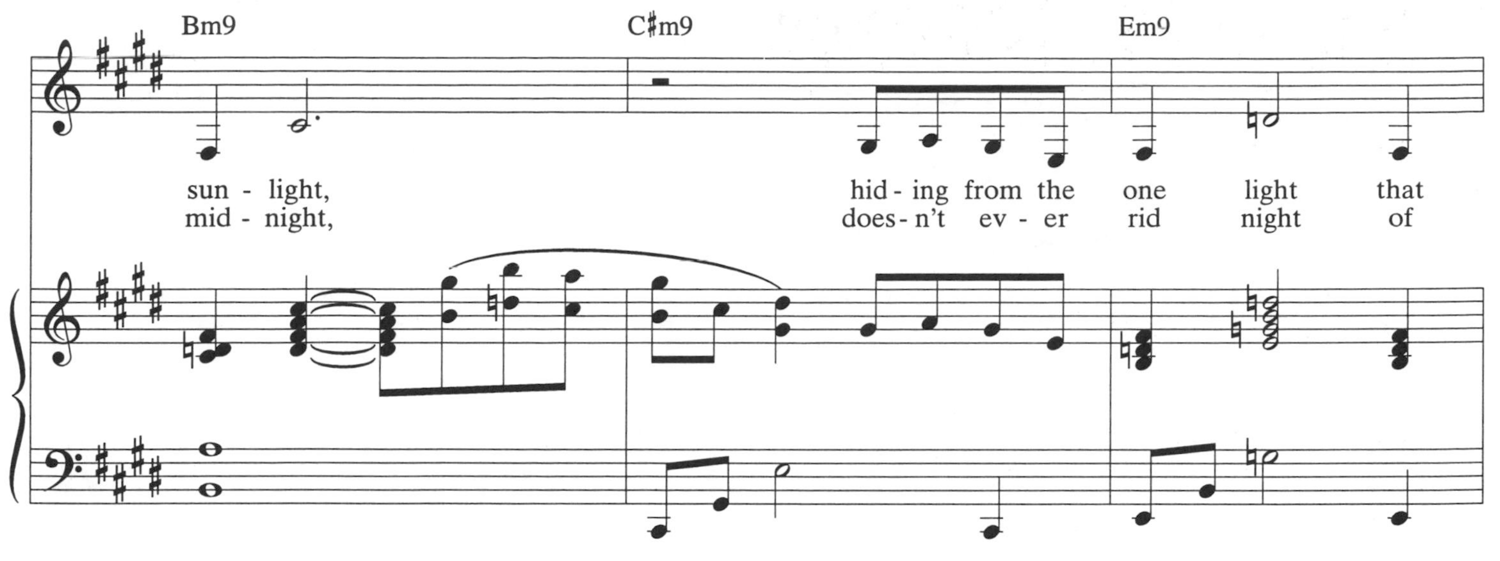
Bm9
C♯m9
Em9
sun - light,
hid - ing from the
one
light
that
mid - night,
does - n't ev - er
rid
night
of

Em7/A
Dmaj9
Am11
D7
might
help
to
guide
you.
Hid - ing from to -
night - mares
as
love
might.
Life is full of

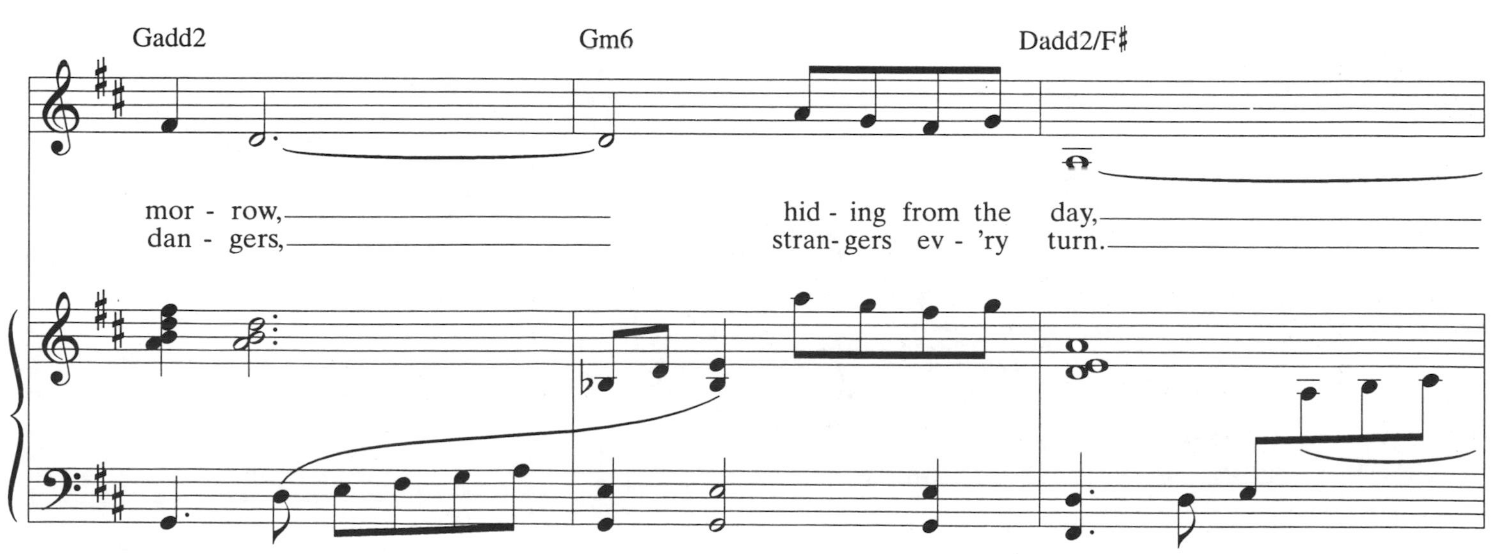
Gadd2
Gm6
Dadd2/F♯
mor - row,
hid - ing from the
day,
dan - gers,
stran - gers ev - 'ry
turn.

Bm7
F♯m7/B
B7♭9
Em9
Em7/A
on - ly brings a sor - row that won't go a -
Liv - ing in the shad - ows, there's no way to
1.
Dadd2
G♯7♯9♯5
way.
2.
D
learn. The
A little faster
F♯m/E
Em7
A/E
F♯m/E
Em7
G/A
A/G
F♯m7
more you learn, the more you seek, the more you find.
mf
Dmaj7
G/F
Fmaj7
G/F
F
G/C
Dm7
The more you care, the more the world is

Tempo I
E7sus4
G♯7♯5
C♯m9
kind.
One thing I can
poco. rit. e dim.
mp
Bm9
C♯m9
Bm9
tell you:
life should be your lov - er,
C♯m9
Em9
Em7/A
help you to dis - cov - er your rea - son for
Dadd2
Am/D
D7
Gadd2
be - ing.
Soon you will be see - ing

C9
F♯m7
Bm7sus4
F♯m7/B
B7♭9
what you're all a - bout.
Liv - ing in the
Em9
Em7/A
A13
Bm9
shad - ows, you'll nev - er find out.
Slowly
D+/A♯
Bm7
Em9
Em7/A
Push a - way the shad - ows, the sun will come
rit.
Tempo I
Bm7
A7
D6
out.
rit.

from GRAND HOTEL

Love Can't Happen

Words and Music by Maury Yeston

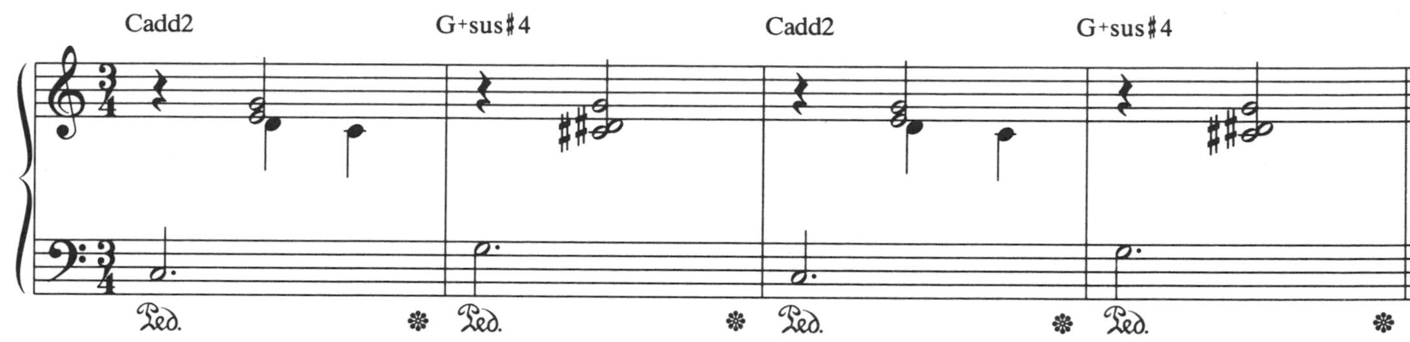

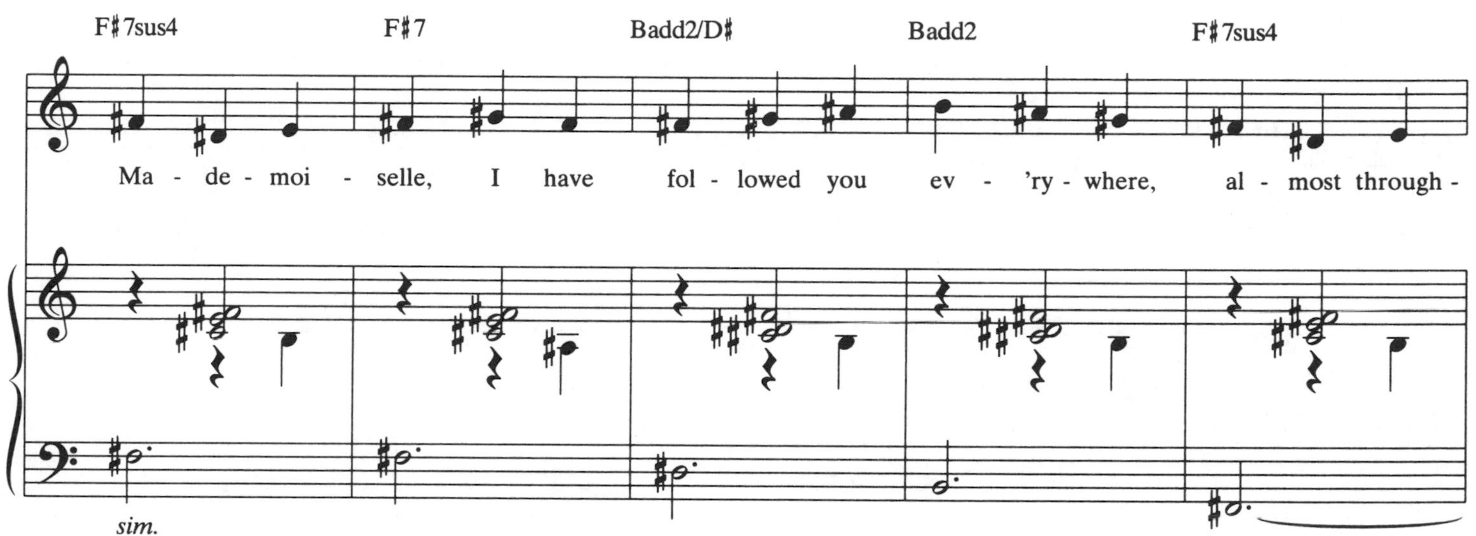

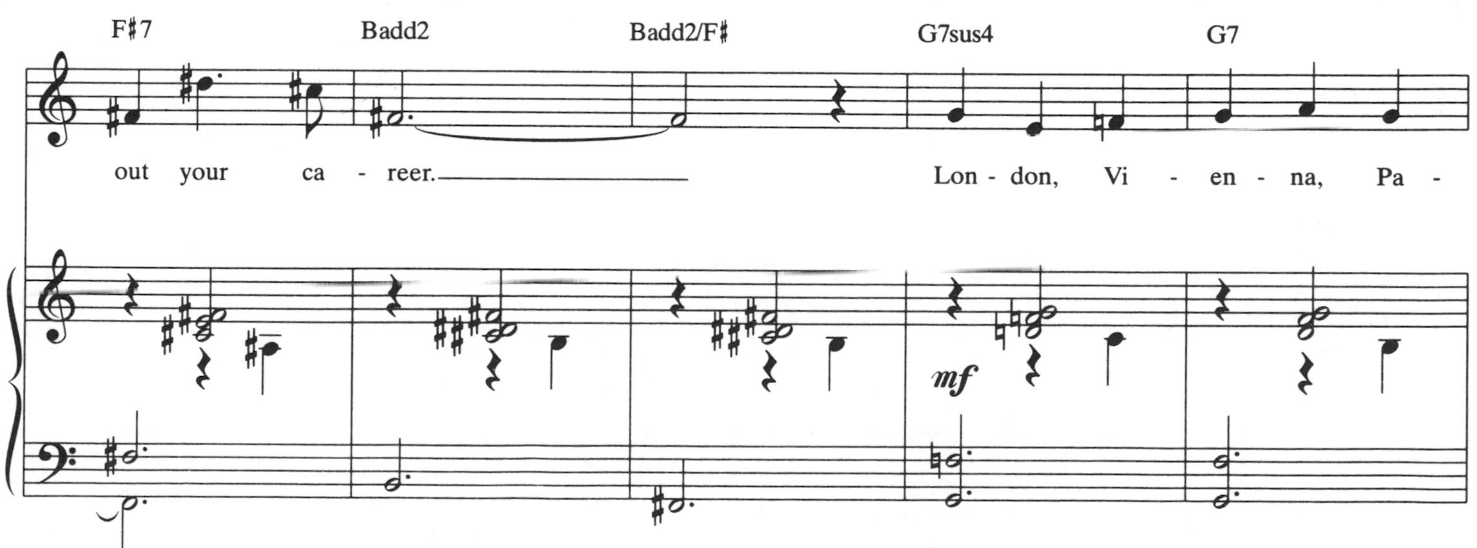

Cadd2
G7sus4
G7
ree, I've ad - mired you, hop - ing one day we might
A♭7sus4
A♭7
G7sus4
G7
A♭7sus4
meet in this way. Though I nev - er thought I'd be car - ried a -
A♭7
B♭7sus4
A♭/C
B♭/D
way, oh, I knew you'd be beau - ti - ful, but not so beau - ti - ful...
cresc.
mf
rit.
B♭/E♭
E♭
B♭/E♭
E♭
B♭/E♭
Love can't hap - pen quite so
mf
a tempo
Ped.
Ped.
Ped.
Ped.

B♭/C
Cm
B♭/C
Cm
Gm/C
quick - ly, not un - less I
sim.
E♭/A♭
A♭
Cm/F
Fm
Fm6
dreamed you, beau - ti - f'ly and
A♭/B♭
B♭
B♭/E♭
sweet - ly...
No,
E♭
B♭/E♭
E♭
B♭/E♭
B♭/C
don't look through me so clear -

Cm
B♭/C
Cm
Gm/C
E♭/A♭
ly.
I
might
ver
-
y
near
-
A♭
E♭/F
Fm
E♭/B♭
ly
lose
my
-
self
com
-
plete
-
cresc.
B♭
Gm/C
Cm
ly.
Who
could
f
Gm/B♭
Cm/B♭
B♭
E♭maj7/A
Am7♭5
ev
-
er
have
sus
-
pect
-
ed

D7
D/G
Gm
you
would
sfz
f
D/F♯
Gm/F♯
D7/F♯
Gm/F♯
B♭/F
make
me
trem
-
ble
so?
5
Em7♭5
D/B♭
Gm/B♭
I
can't
D/B♭
Gm
D/B♭
Gm/B♭
C°7
Gm/D
think
of
an
-
y
an
-
swer
cresc.

D/E♭
E♭
C/E
B♭/F
Cm9
Cm
oth - er
than, if
love
comes...
Ped.
Cm9
Gm/F
E♭/F
When
love
comes,
F7sus4
E♭/F
F/B♭
B♭
you
know.
mf

G
F/G
Cadd2
G+sus♯4
What is this I'm say- ing? What is this I'm
dim.
mp
feel - ing?
Like I'm get- ting drunk, look- ing in her
eyes...
A♭7sus4
A♭7
D♭add2/F
O - ver- whelm- ing face, ut- ter- ly ap - peal - ing.
mf
D♭add2
C♭13
G♭add2/B♭
Nev- er mind the truth, nev- er mind the lies. Nev- er mind a
cresc.

G♭/A♭
A♭/D♭
D♭
thought in the world ex - cept...
Love can't
mf
A♭/D♭
D♭
A♭/D♭
A♭/B♭
B♭m
hap - pen quite so quick - ly,
A♭/B♭
B♭m
Fm/B♭
D♭/G♭
G♭
B♭m/E♭
E♭m
I might ver - y near - ly lose my -
D♭/A♭
A♭
self com - plete - ly.
ff

Fm/B♭
B♭m
Fm/A♭
B♭m/A♭
A♭
Who could ev - er have sus -
D♭maj7/G
Gm7♭5
C7
pect - ed
sfz
C/F
Fm
C/E
Fm/E
C7/E
Fm/E
I would be here trem - bling
A♭/E♭
Dm7♭5
so?
5

C/A♭ Fm/A♭ C/A♭ Fm/A♭ C/A♭ Fm/A♭
I can't think of an - y
B♭°7 Fm/C C/D♭ D♭ B♭/D A♭/E♭
an - swer oth - er than, if
B♭m9 B♭m
love comes, when
Fm/E♭ D♭/E♭ E♭7sus4
love comes, you

E♭/A♭
A♭
E♭/A♭
A♭
E♭/A♭
E♭/F
know.
f
cresc.
Fm7
D♭/E♭
A♭7sus4
E♭/A♭
And
I
know!
ff
A♭
E♭/A♭
A♭
E♭/F
Fm
D♭/E♭
A♭7sus4
A♭

from MAME

Mame

Music and Lyric by Jerry Herman

A9
Dm
Dm(+7)
Dm7
G7
G9+5
band, The whole plan - ta - tion's hum - min' since
speech, You may be from Man-hat - tan, but
C
C#dim
Dm7
G7
C
C6
you brought Dix - ie back to Dix - ie - land. You make the
Geor - gia nev - er had a sweet - er peach. You make our
Cmaj7
C#dim
Dm7
G7
Dm
Dm(+7)
cot - ton eas - y to pick, Mame,
black - eyed peas and our grits, Mame,
You give my
Seem like the
Dm7
G7
E7
Dm6
E7
Am
Am(+7)
old mint ju - lep a kick, Mame,
bill of fare at the Ritz, Mame,
You make the
You came, you
3

Am7
Ebdim
Em
A9
old mag - no - lia tree blos - som at the men - tion of your name,
saw, you con - quered and ab - so - lute - ly noth - ing is the same.
Dm
Dm(+7)
Dm7
G7
Em
Em(+7)
Em7
You've made us feel a - live a - gain, You've giv - en
Your spe - cial fas - ci - na - tion 'll Prove to be
A9
D7
Dm7
G7
G7-9
us the drive a - gain, To make the South re - vive a - gain,
in - spi - ra - tion - al, We think you're just sen - sa - tion - al,
C
Cdim
Dm7
G7
C
Mame.
Mame.

from MAN OF LA MANCHA

Man Of La Mancha (I, Don Quixote)

Lyric by Joe Darion
Music by Mitch Leigh

Gm F A A7 Gm6 A7
hurls down his gaunt - let to thee! I am
vir - tue shall tri - umph at last! I am
f
D A D A
I, Don Qui - xo - te, the Lord of La Man - cha, De -
I, Don Qui - xo - te, the Lord of La Man - cha, My
Bm F♯m Em7 A Am
- stroy - er of e - vil am I. I will
des - ti - ny calls and I go. And the
Dm Am Dm Am
march to the sound of the trum - pets Of glo - ry for -
wild winds of for - tune will car - ry me on - ward oh
mf

1.
2.
Tag
Dm
C7
F
Am
Dm
- ev - er to con - quer or die!
whith - er so -
2. Hear me,
mf
F
Am
Dm
- ev - er they blow.
Dm
Whith - er so - ev - er they blow,
mf
F
Am
rall.
Dm
Am7
Dm
On - ward to glo - ry I go!
f
fz
rall.

from THE CIVIL WAR: AN AMERICAN MUSICAL

Missing You (My Bill)

Words by Jack Murphy
Music by Frank Wildhorn

G
B♭
Bm
Dm
And Bil - ly helped and scraped his knee,
You al - ways meant to get to it,
C
E♭
G/D
B♭/F
D
F
B
D
but he took it all in stride.
but I know you had to leave.
Em
Gm
G7
B♭7
C
E♭
F7(♭5)
A♭7(♭5)
Day by day I get by, mak - ing do the best I can.
Thank God there's so much to do. It's the work that gets me through.
C/D
E♭/F
D
F
Chorus:
G
B♭
C
E♭
When the sun slow - ly sets just be - hind
mf

D/F♯ G C D/F♯
F/A B♭ E♭ F/A
our hill, then the mem - o - ries come in the eve -
G C
B♭ E♭
ning chill. How I long for your touch like a
D/F♯ Em Cmaj7
F/A Gm E♭maj7
lov - er will! Oh, I'm miss - ing you. God, I'm
1.
C/D D Cmaj9 D/C Cmaj9 D/C C/D
E♭/F F E♭maj9 F/E♭ E♭maj9 F/E♭ E♭/F
miss-ing you, my Bill.

2.
Bridge:
G
B♭
F
A♭
C/E
E♭/G
So I count the days, and I think of ways to
G
D/G
G
B♭
F/B♭
B♭
Gsus
G
B♭sus
B♭
speed them by.
When the
F
A♭
C/E
E♭/G
day is through, I re - mem - ber you and cry.
C/D
E♭/F
D
F
When the

Chorus:
G C D/F♯ G C D/F♯
B♭ E♭ F/A B♭ E♭ F/A
sun slow-ly sets just be-hind our hill, then the mem-o-ries come in the eve-
G C D/F♯ Em
B♭ E♭ F/A Gm
ning chill. How I long for your touch like a lov-er will! Oh, I'm
mp
Cmaj7 C/D D
E♭maj7 E♭/F F N.C.
miss-ing you. God, I'm miss-ing you, my Bill.
Cmaj9 D/C Cmaj9 D/C D7sus G
E♭maj9 F/E♭ E♭maj9 F/E♭ F7sus B♭
rit.

from NINE

My Husband Makes Movies

Words and Music by Maury Yeston

Briskly (♩=84)

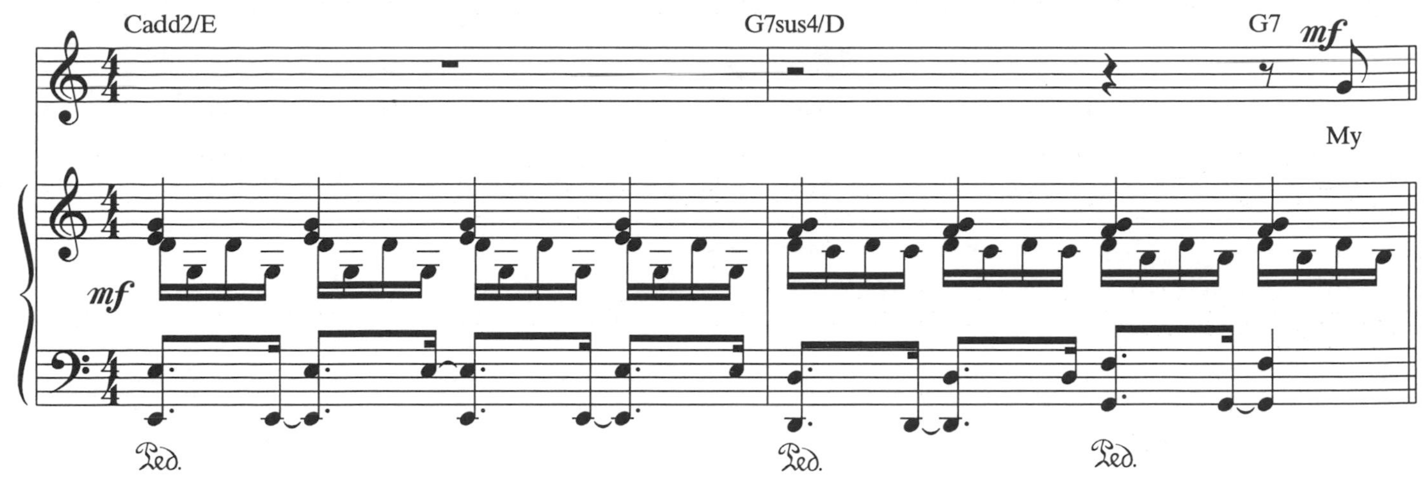

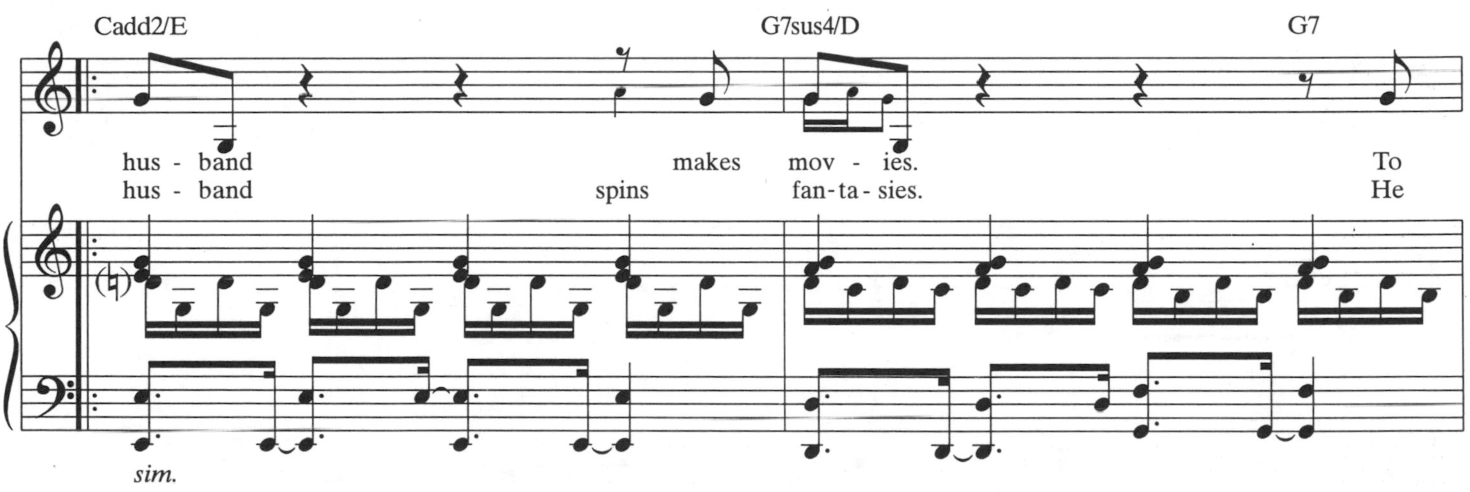

F♯m7♭5
B7
Em
Emadd2/D
ac - tions aren't al - ways what they seem. He may be
work - ing on the film on an - cient Rome, he made the
Am7
C/D
D7
G
B7
on to some u - nique ro - man - tic theme.
slave girls take the glad - i - a - tors home!
Em
Emadd2/D
C♯m7♭5
Gmaj7/D
Some men catch fish, some men tie flies,
Some men buy stocks, some men punch clocks,
Em
Emadd2/D
C♯m7♭5
some earn their liv - ing bak - ing bread. My
some leap where oth - ers fear to tread. My

G/D
Am7/D
D7
hus - band, he goes a lit - tle cra - zy, mak - ing
hus - band, as au - thor and di - rec - tor, makes up
1.
Dm7♭5/G
Dm7/G
B♭add2/G
G7
G7sus4
G7♭5
G7
G7♯5
mov - ies in - stead. My
2.
Dm7♭5/G
Dm7/G
B♭add2/G
G7
G7sus4
G7♭5
G7
G7♯5
sto - ries in his head.
Cmadd2/E♭
G7(no3)/D
G7/B
Cmadd2/E♭
rit.
mp
rit.

Tempo II
Slower (♩=68)
Cmadd2/E♭
G7(no3)/D
Cmadd2/E♭
mp
G7(no3)/D
G7/B
Gui- do Con- ti - ni, Lu - i - sa Con - ti - ni:
Cmadd2/E♭
G7(no3)/D
G7/B
A♭/C
B♭7/D
num - ber one gen- ius and num - ber one fan.
Gui- do Con- ti - ni, Lu- i - sa Con- ti - ni:
A♭/C
B♭7/D
E♭maj7
A♭maj7
daugh-ter of well - to- do Flor- en- tine clan long a - go, twen- ty years a -
Dm7♭5
rit.
G7sus4
G7
Cmadd2/E♭
a tempo
G7(no3)/D
G7/B
go. Once the names were Gui- do Con- ti - ni, Lu - i - sa Del For- no:
rit.
a tempo

Cmadd2/E♭
G7(no3)/D
G7/B
A♭/C
B♭7/D
ac - tress with dreams and a life of her own. Pas-sion-ate, wild, and in love in Li-vor-no,
A♭/C
B♭7/D
E♭maj7
A♭maj7
sing-ing with Gui-do all night on the phone long a - go, some-one else a -
Dm7♭5
G7sus4
G7
F♯°7
Fm7♭5/G♯
rit.
go. How he needs me so, and he'll be the
Tempo I
Cmadd2/G Cm/G Dm7♭5/G G Cmadd2/E♭
G7sus4 Dm7♭5/G G7sus4 G7
mf
last to know it. My hus - band makes mov - ies. To

Fm9
B♭7sus4
B♭7
E♭add2
E♭add2/D
make them, he makes him - self ob-sessed. He works for
Dm7♭5
G7
Cmadd2
Cmadd2/B♭
weeks on end with-out a bit of rest. No oth - er
Fm7
B♭7sus4
B♭7
E♭add2
G7/B
way can he a-chieve his lev- el best.
Cmadd2/E♭
G7(no3)/D
G7/B
Cmadd2/E♭
G7(no3)/D
G7/B
Some men read books, some shine their shoes,

Gm7♭5/B♭
C7
Fmadd2
Fm/E♭
some re-tire ear - ly when they've seen the eve - ning news. My
B♭m7
D♭/E♭
A♭maj9
A♭/G
hus - band on - ly rare - ly comes to bed. My
Dm7♭5
G7sus4
G7
rit.
hus - band makes mov - ies in - stead. My
rit.
Slower (♩=68)
Cadd2/E
G7sus4/D
G7
Cadd2
hus - band makes mov - ies.
8va

from THE SOUND OF MUSIC

My Favorite Things

Lyrics by Oscar Hammerstein II
Music by Richard Rodgers

Em
Cream col - ored pon - ies and crisp ap - ple
mf
mp
Cmaj7
strud - els, Door - bells and sleigh - bells and schnitz - el with noo - dles,
Am7
D7
G/B
C/E
G/D
Wild geese that fly with the moon on their wings, These are a
C
F♯m7♭5
4fr
B7
E
few of my fa - vor - ite things.
f

A
Girls in white dress - es with blue sat - in sash - es, Snow - flakes that
mf
Am7
D7
stay on my nose and eye - lash - es, Sil - ver white win - ters that
G/B
C/E
G/D
C
F#m7b5
4fr
B7b9
melt in - to springs, These are a few of my fa - vor - ite things.
Em
F#m7b5
4fr
B7
When the dog bites, When the bee stings,
mf

Em
C
When I'm feel - ing sad, I
A7/C♯
A7
sim - ply re - mem - ber my fa - vor - ite things and
G/D
C/D
G/D
C/D
G
D7♭9
4fr
D7
G
then I don't feel so bad.
cresc.
f
C
G/D
D7
G
sf

from PHANTOM

My True Love

Words and Music by Maury Yeston

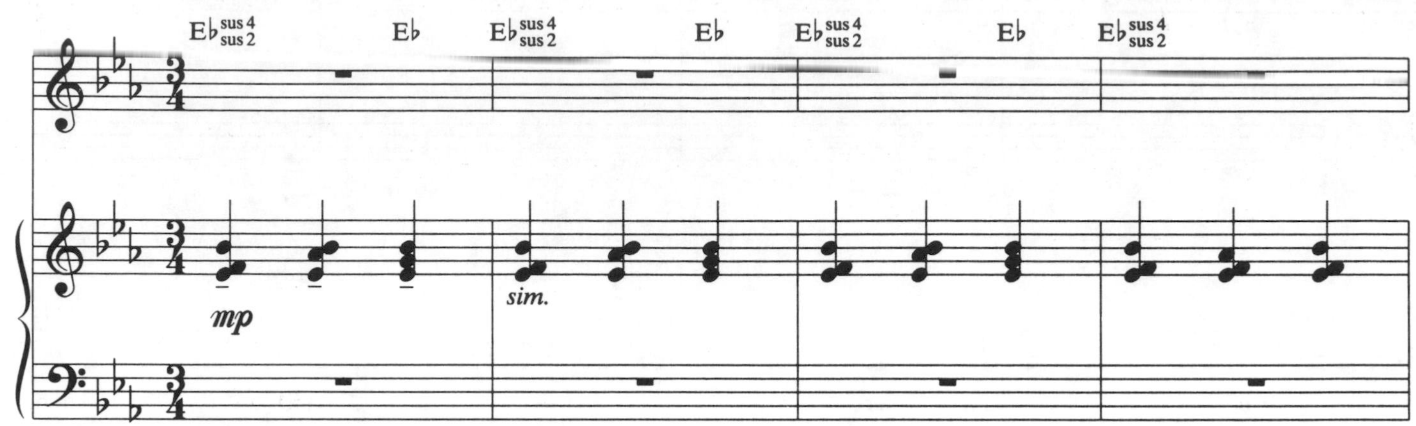

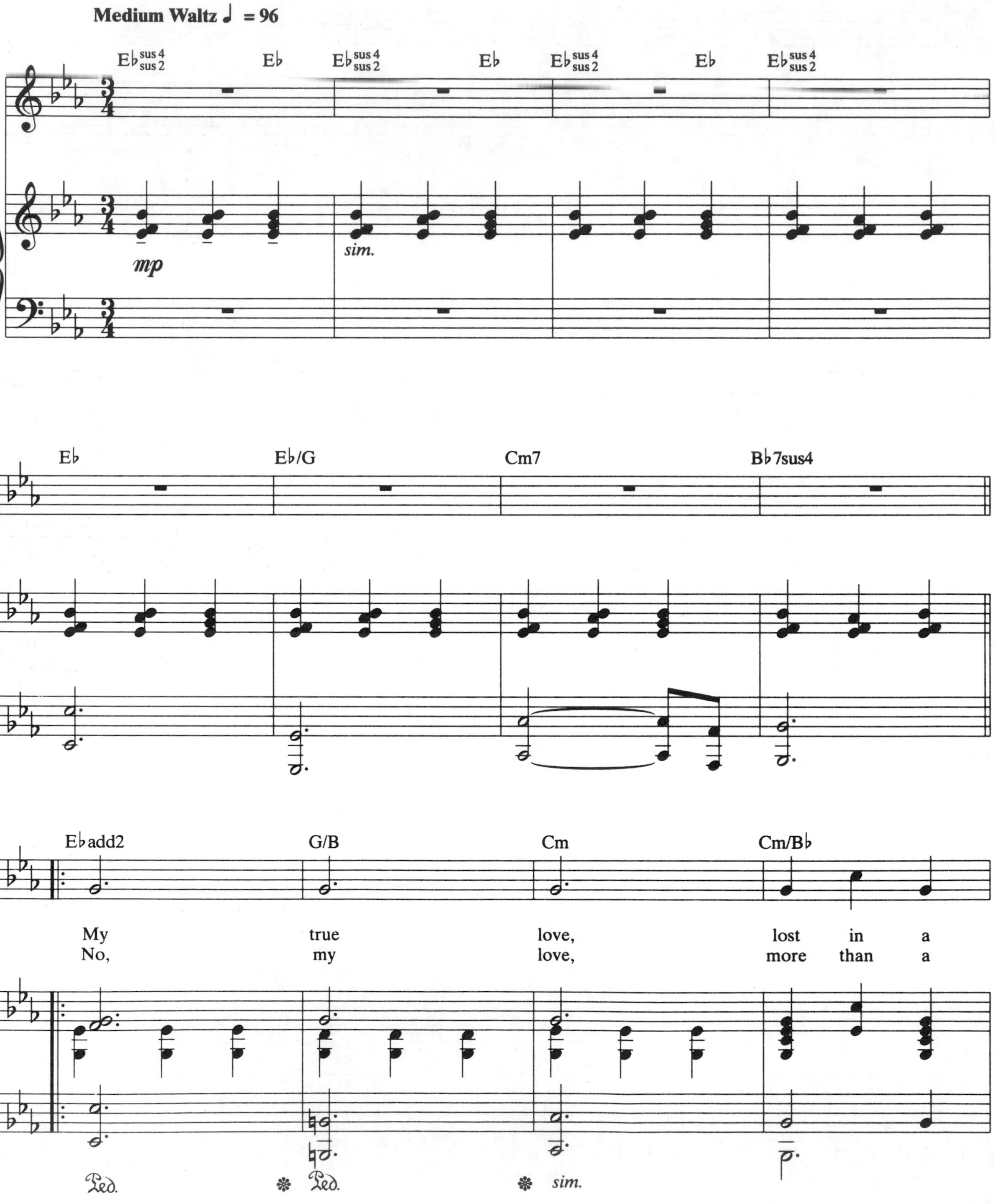

E♭ E♭/G Cm7 B♭7sus4

E♭add2 G/B Cm Cm/B♭

My true love, lost in a

No, my love, more than a

Ped. ✽ Ped. ✽ sim.

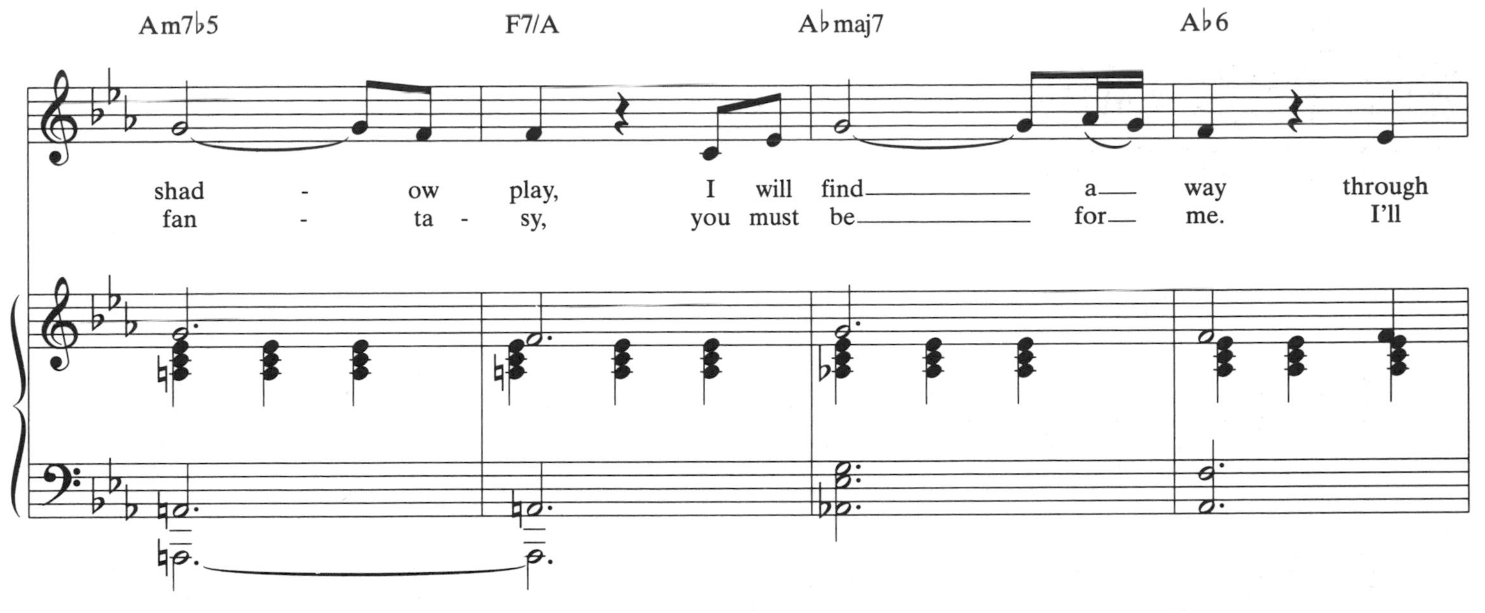
Am7♭5
F7/A
A♭maj7
A♭6
shad - ow play, I will find a way through
fan - ta - sy, you must be for me. I'll

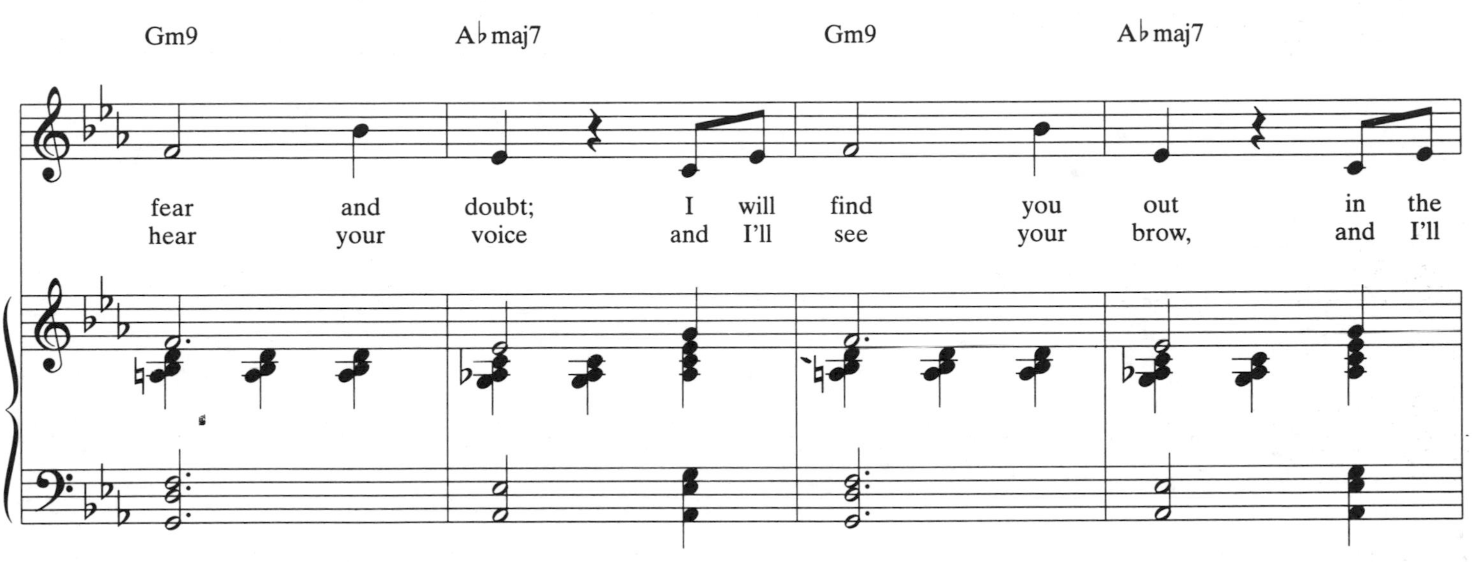
Gm9
A♭maj7
Gm9
A♭maj7
fear and doubt; I will find you out in the
hear your voice and I'll see your brow, and I'll

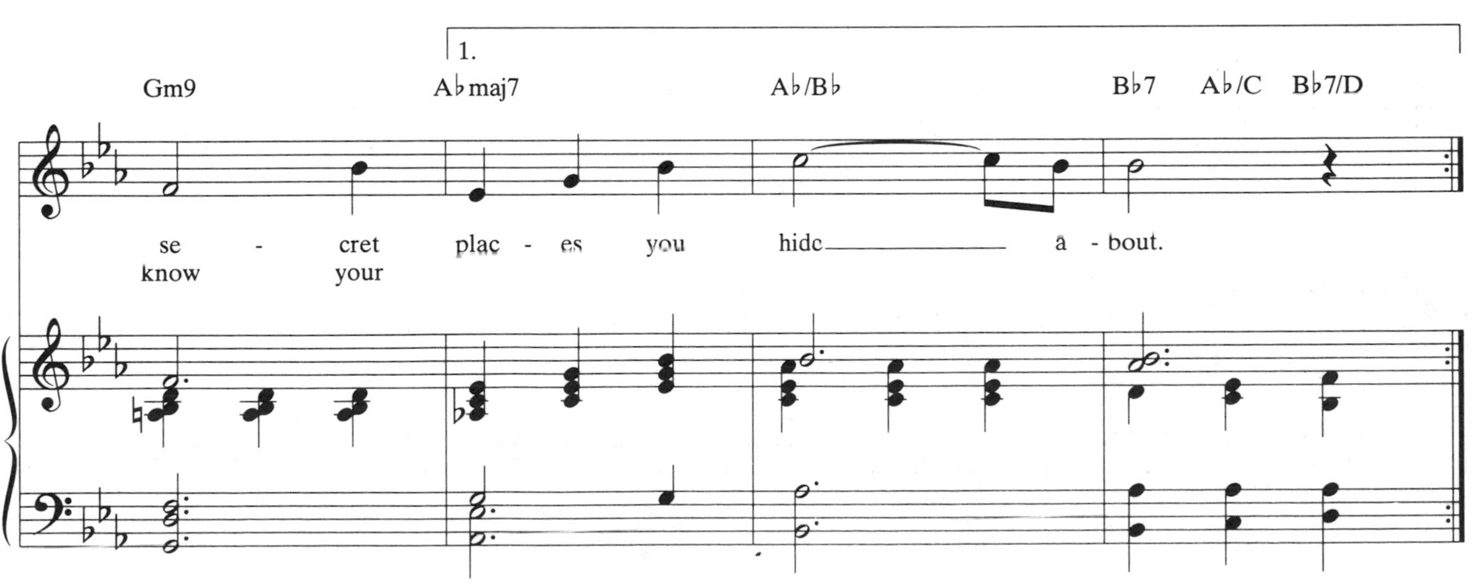
1.
Gm9
A♭maj7
A♭/B♭
B♭7
A♭/C
B♭7/D
se - cret plac - es you hide a - bout.
know your

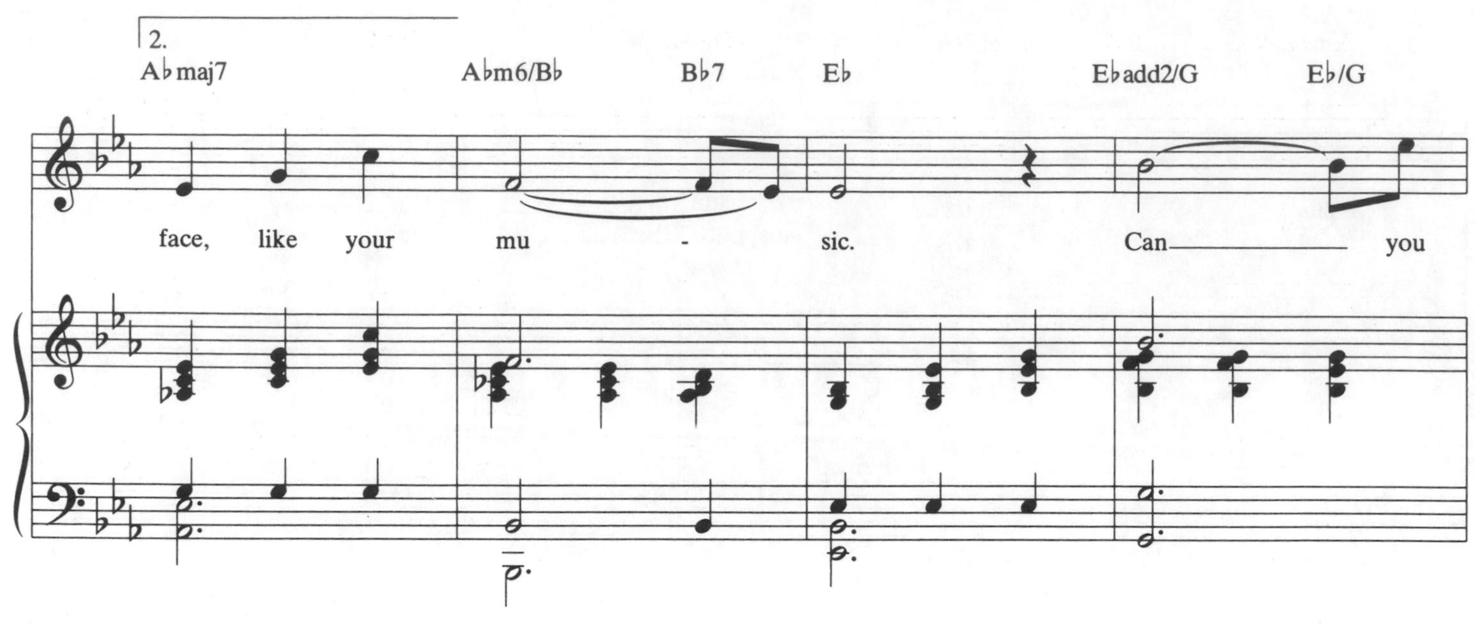
2.
A♭maj7
A♭m6/B♭
B♭7
E♭
E♭add2/G
E♭/G
face, like your mu - sic. Can you

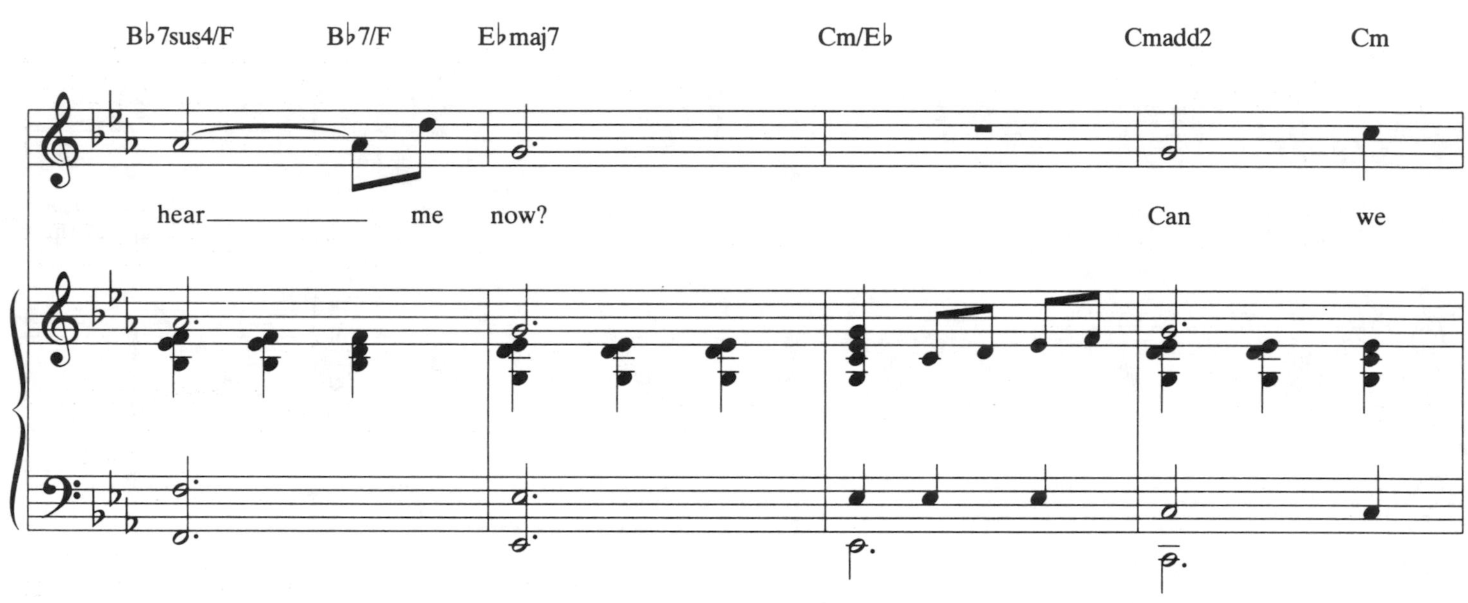
B♭7sus4/F
B♭7/F
E♭maj7
Cm/E♭
Cmadd2
Cm
hear me now? Can we

G7sus4
G7
Cm
E♭7
E♭7sus4/F
E♭7/G
A♭
make a vow ev - er

E♭7sus4/A♭ E♭7/A♭ Fm Fm9 Dm7♭5 E♭add2
to be faith - ful? I will
B♭7sus4/A♭ B♭7 E♭7sus4 E♭7 E♭7sus4/F E♭7/G A♭
show you how. My
mf
C/E Dm7(no5) C/E Fm Cm(no5)/E♭ B♭m(no5)/E♭ A♭/E♭ Dm7♭5
true love, o - pen and turn to
B♭7/D D♭maj7 D♭6 Cm9
me what no one can see, your deep - est

D♭maj7
Cm9
D♭maj7
Cm9
dreams of your dark - est nights, and your eyes like
D♭maj7
E♭7sus4
E♭7
A♭
Cm9
lights ev - er burn - ing. I will hear your
f
D♭maj7
Cm9
D♭maj7
Cm9
voice and I'll see your brow and I'll know your
D♭maj7
E♭7sus4
E♭7
A♭
face. Let me know it now,
ff

A♭/C
A♭/F
E♭7sus4
A♭
now.
A♭/C
A♭/F
E♭7sus4
B♭
My
fff
D7
Gm
Dm(no5)/F
Cm(no5)/F
B♭/F
Em7♭5
true
love,
lost
in
a
shad
-
ow
C7/E
E♭maj7
E♭6
Dm9
play,
I
will
find
a
way
through
fear
and

E♭maj7
Dm9
E♭maj7
Dm9
doubt, I will find you out. Let me know your
E♭maj7
F7sus4
F7
B♭
face, let me know it now,
B♭/D
B♭/G
F7sus4
B♭
B♭/D
now,
ff
B♭/G
F7sus4
B♭
now.
rit.
fff

from JEKYLL & HYDE

A New Life

Words by Leslie Bricusse
Music by Frank Wildhorn

Moderately slow, freely

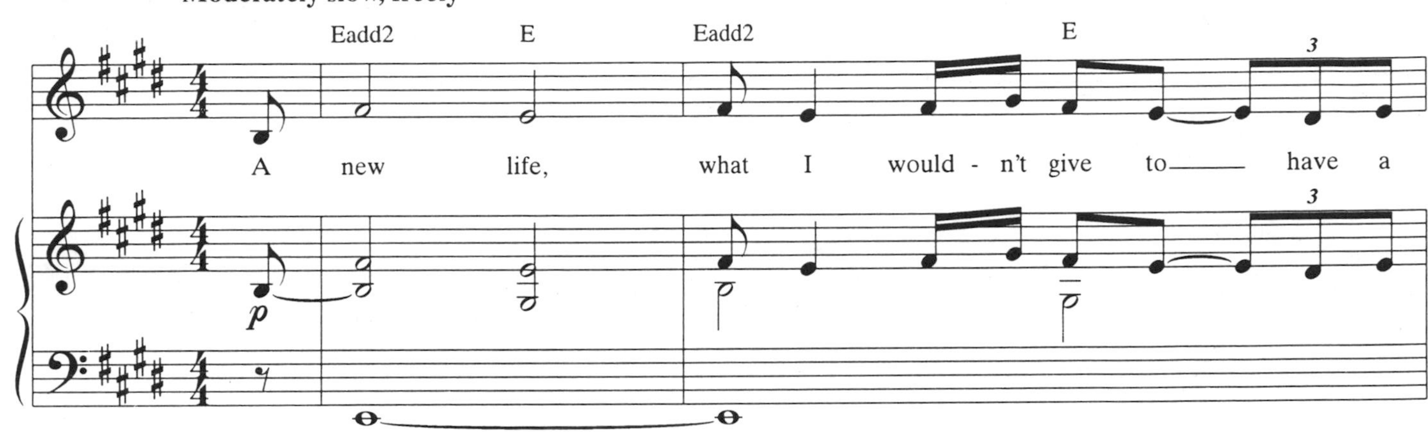

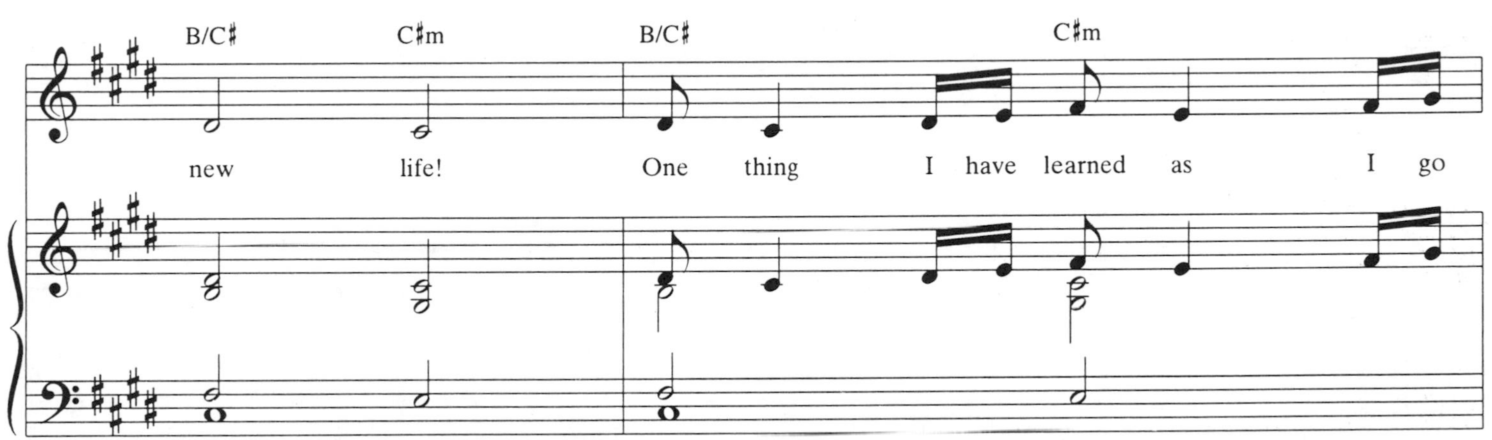

Eadd2
E
Eadd2
E
new start, that's the thing I need to give me
B/C♯
C♯m
B/C♯
C♯m
new heart. Half a chance in life to find a
F♯m7
F♯m7♭5
new part, just a sim - ple role that I can
F♯m7/B
E/D
D
E/D
play. A new hope, some - thing to con - vince me to re -
3
3

A
new hope!
A
E/D D E/D
A
new day, bright e - nough to help me find my way!
A
D♯m7
G♯7♭9
B/C♯ C♯m
new chance, one that may - be has a touch of ro - mance.
F♯7
F♯m7
F♯m7/B
Where can it be, the chance for me?
A

Moderately, in rhythm
Eadd2
E
Eadd2
E
new dream,
I have one I know that very - y
mp
B/C♯
C♯m
B/C♯
C♯m
few dream!
I would like to see that o - ver -
F♯m7
F♯m7♭5
due dream,
e - ven though it nev - er may come
F♯m7/B
Eadd2
E
true! A new love,

Eadd2
E
B/C♯
C♯m
though I know there's no such thing as true love.
B/C♯
C♯m
F♯m7
E - ven so, al - though I nev - er knew love,
F♯m7♭5
Bsus4
G♯m/B
A/B
F♯m
F♯m/B
still I feel that one dream is my due!
A
Gadd2
G
Gadd2
G
D/E
Em
new world, this one thing I want to ask of you, world.
mf

D/E
Em
Am7
Once! Be - fore it's time to say a - dieu, world!
Am7♭5
Dsus4
C/D
Dsus4
One sweet chance to prove the cyn - ics wrong! A
D/G
G
D/G
G
new life, more and more I'm sure as I go
D/E
Em
D/E
Em7
through life. Just to play the game and to pur -

Am7
Dsus4 sus2
B/D♯
sue life, just to share its pleas - ures and be -
Em7
A7
Am7
B7
long! That's what I've been here for all a -
cresc.
Em7
A7
Am7
C/D
Gadd2
long! Each day's a brand - new life!
f
D/E
Em
D/E
Em7
Cmaj9/F
Cmaj9
G
rit.

from TITANIC

No Moon

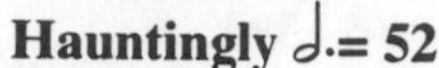

Music and Lyrics by Maury Yeston

Hauntingly ♩. = 52

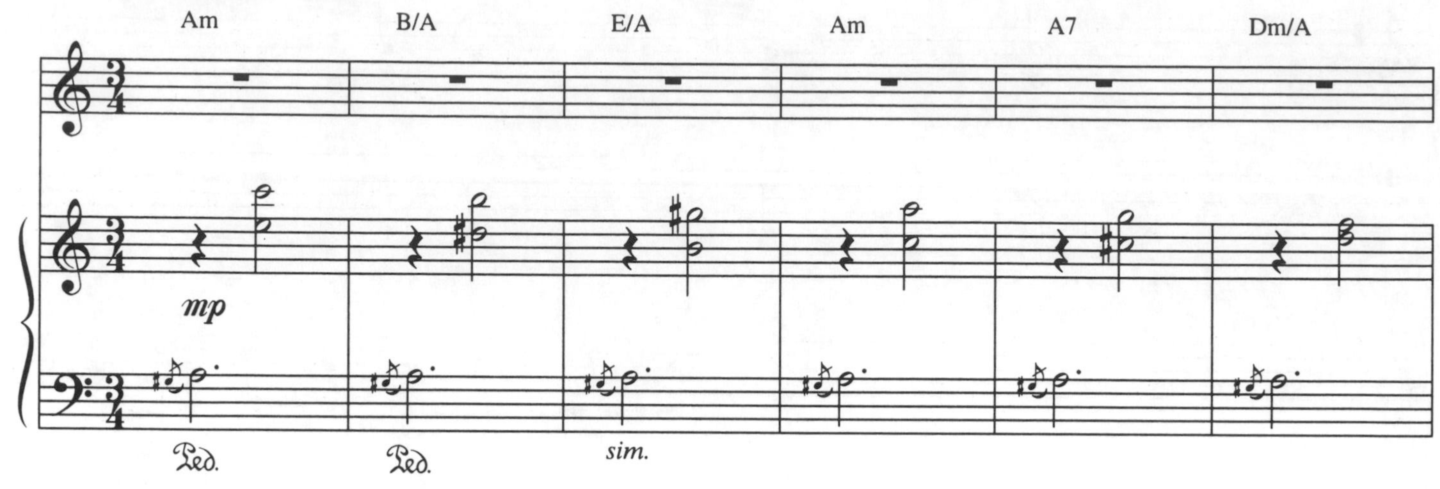

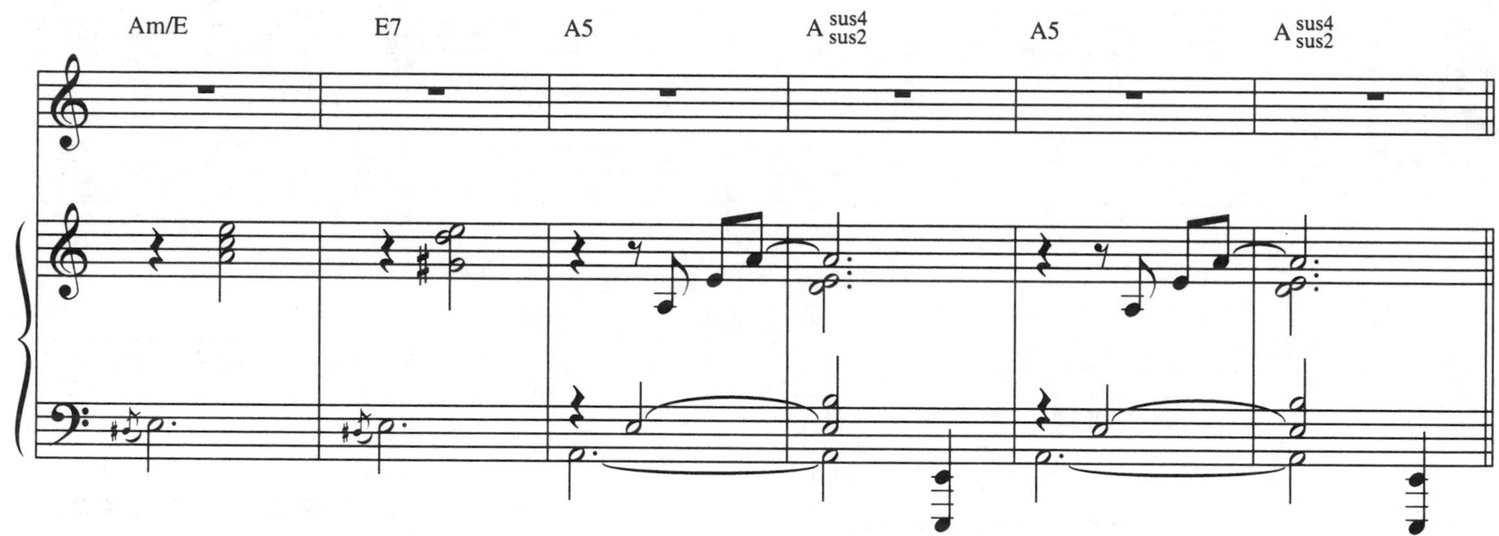

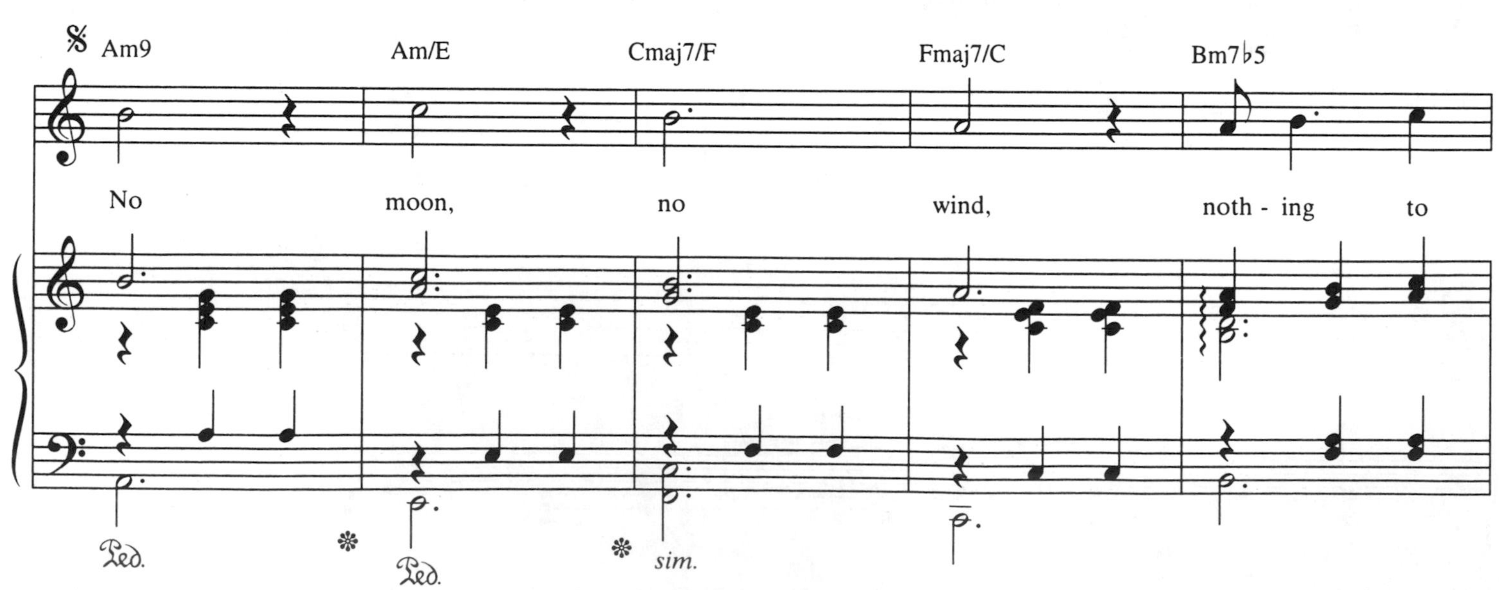

Em7
Fmaj9
Fmaj7/C
spy things by.
No wave,
Dm9sus4
Dm
Bm7♭5
E7sus4
E7
no swell, no line where sea meets sky.
G/A
Am/E
G/F
F/C
Dm7
Still - ness, dark - ness. "Can't see a
G7
C
Fmaj9
Bm7♭5
G♯°7
thing," says I. No re - flec - tion, not a

Am F♯m7♭5 B♭ Am/E E7 Am A sus4 sus2
shad - ow, not a glint of light meets the eye.
A5 A sus4 sus2 A Asus4 Em7
And we go sail - ing, sail -
C/E Dm7 Bm7♭5/D E Am
ing ev - er west - ward on the sea. We go
Fmaj7 G7 C F Bm7♭5
sail - ing, sail - ing, ev - er

Am/E
E7
Am
B/A
E/A
Am
on go we...
mp
A7
Dm/A
Am/E
E7
To Coda
A5
Asus4 sus2
p
A5
Asus4 sus2
Dm6/A
Amadd2
A - head we plow
Dm/A
Amadd2
in - to the dark - en - ing night. Can't

G9
Amadd2
see
the
bow...
How
then
to
cresc.
Fmaj7♯5
F°7
Am/E
Esus4
search
with
on
-
ly
Fmaj9
E7♭9
D.S. al Coda
star
-
light?
Coda
A5
Am
poco rit.

from OKLAHOMA!

Oh, What A Beautiful Mornin'

Lyrics by Oscar Hammerstein II
Music by Richard Rodgers

Abm/Cb
Eb/Bb
Bb7/Ab
Eb/G
The corn is as high as an el - e - phant's
They don't turn their heads as they see me ride
The breeze is so bus - y it don't miss a
Ab
Eb
eye, an' it looks like it's climb - in' clear
by, but a lit - tle brown mav' - rick is
tree, and a ol' weep - in' wil - ler is
mf
Bbdim
Bb7
Eb
up to the sky.
wink - in' her eye.
laugh - in' at me!
Oh, what a beau - ti - ful
mp
Absus
Ab
Eb
morn - in'.
Oh, what a beau - ti - ful

B♭7
E♭
3fr
day.
I got a beau - ti - ful
A♭
4fr
Adim
E♭
B♭7
feel - in'.
Ev - 'ry - thing's go - in' my
1, 2
E♭
B♭7
3
Fm7/B♭
way.
All the
All the
way.
p
riten.
Oh, what a beau - ti - ful day!

from THOROUGHLY MODERN MILLIE

Not For The Life Of Me

Music by Jeanine Tesori
Lyrics by Dick Scanlan

D9sus4 D7♭9 D7 G/D C7 G/D C7♯5
you. You cer - tain - ly are dif - f'rent from what they have back home, where
G F/A B♭7 G/B G7/B C
noth - ing's o - ver three sto - ries high, and no one's in a hur - ry or
E♭9♯11 E♭7 G/D D°7 Am7 D7
wants to roam, but I do, though they won - der why. They
p sub.
B9 B♭7 C/G Am6 B♭7
said I would soon be good and lone - ly. They said I would sing the home - sick
mp

Ebmadd2
Ebm
Ebo7
F7/Eb
Bb/D
blues. So I al - ways have this tick - et in my pock - et, a tick - et
F#m7b5
Slower
Tacet
A7b5
Eb7/Bb
home in my pock - et to do with as I choose.
Hot Dixieland
Tacet
Ab6
Tacet
Eb7#5
Ab7
Burn the bridge. Bet the store. Ba - by's com - in' home
f
Db7
Bb7
Eb7
Ab6
Bo7
no more. Not for the life of me.

Gm7b5/Bb
Eb+
Ab
Ab6
Tacet
Eb7#5
Break the lock.
Post my bail.
Ab7
Db7
Bb7
Done my time, I'm out - ta jail.
Not for the
Eb7
Ab
Ab7
Abo7
Bbm7b5/Ab
Ab
life of me.
A life that's
Em6
B7
Em6
B7
Em6
C7
got - ta be more than a one - light town where the light is al - ways red.
got - ta be more than a coun - try wife mak - in' ba - bies till I croak.

Em6
E7
Got - ta be more___ than an old ghost town where the
Got - ta be more___ than the lead - ing role in a
A7
Bb7
Eb9
ghost ain't e - ven dead.
far - mer's daugh - ter joke.
Ab6
Eb9
Cm7b5
Ab7
Clap - a - your hands___ just - a - be - cause don't you know that where I am ain't
Days of yore,___ kind and gen - tle, ask me if I'm
Db7
Bb7
Eb9
where I was.___
sen - ti - men - tal.
Not for the life of

Cm7b5
F7
Bb7
me.
Boh doh dee oh.
Not for the
Not for the
Eb7
1.
Ab Ab7 Ab°7 Bbm7b5/Ab
Ab
life of
life of,
me.
You see, I
2.
Ab7
Db D°7
Ab/Eb
E7
not for the life of,
not for the life
Eb9
Ab Bb
Ab7#5 D(b5)
Ab
of
me!
L.H.

from LES MISÉRABLES

On My Own

Music by Claude-Michel Schönberg
Lyrics by Alain Boublil, John Caird, Trevor Nunn, Jean-Marc Natel and Herbert Kretzmer

G
F#7
Bm
him I feel his arms a - round me. And
dark - ness the trees are full of star - light. And
Em
Em/D
1
A
when I lose my way I close my eyes and he has found me. In the
all I see is him and me for - ev - er and for-
2
A
Bb
Ebm/Bb
ev - er. And I know it's on - ly in my
mf
più mosso
Bb
Bb/A
Gm
Gm/F
mind that I'm talk - ing to my - self and not to

Eb
Em
him. And al - though I know that he is
B
B7
Am7
C7
blind, Still I say there's a way for us. I
F
Gm/F
F
F/E
love him, but when the night is o - ver, he is
mf
Dm
G7
C
C/B
gone, the ri - ver's just a ri - ver. With -

B♭
A
Dm
out him the world a-round me chang-es. The
Gm
Gm/F
C
trees are bare and ev-'ry-where the streets are full of strang-ers. I
F
Gm/F
F
F/E
love him but ev-'ry day I'm learn-ing all my
Dm
G7
C
C/B
life I've on-ly been pre-tend-ing. With-

B♭
A
Dm
out me his world will go on turn - ing. The
Gm
C
world is full of hap - pi - ness that I have nev - er known. I
p
F(add9)
F7/E♭
love him, I love him, I
Dm7
B♭m/D♭
F
love him, but on - ly on my own.
rall.

from A CHORUS LINE

One

Music by Marvin Hamlisch
Lyric by Edward Kleban

Am7-5
D7
One smile and sud- den- ly no- bod- y
Gm
D7
Gm
G#m7-5
else will do, You know you'll
C#7
F#m
C#7/E#
A7/E
A7
nev- er be lone- ly with you know who.
Ebmaj7
One mo- ment in her pres- ence
A7
and you can for- get the rest,

Abmaj7
Am7-5
D7
Gm
For the girl is sec- ond best to none,
cresc.
G7
C7
F7
Bb7
son, Ooh! Sigh! Give her your at- ten- tion,
f
Gm7
C7
F7
do I real- ly have to men- tion she's
Bb7
Ebmaj7
Fm7
the one?
mf
Ebmaj7
Fm7
Repeat and Fade.

from NINE

Only With You

Words and Music by Maury Yeston

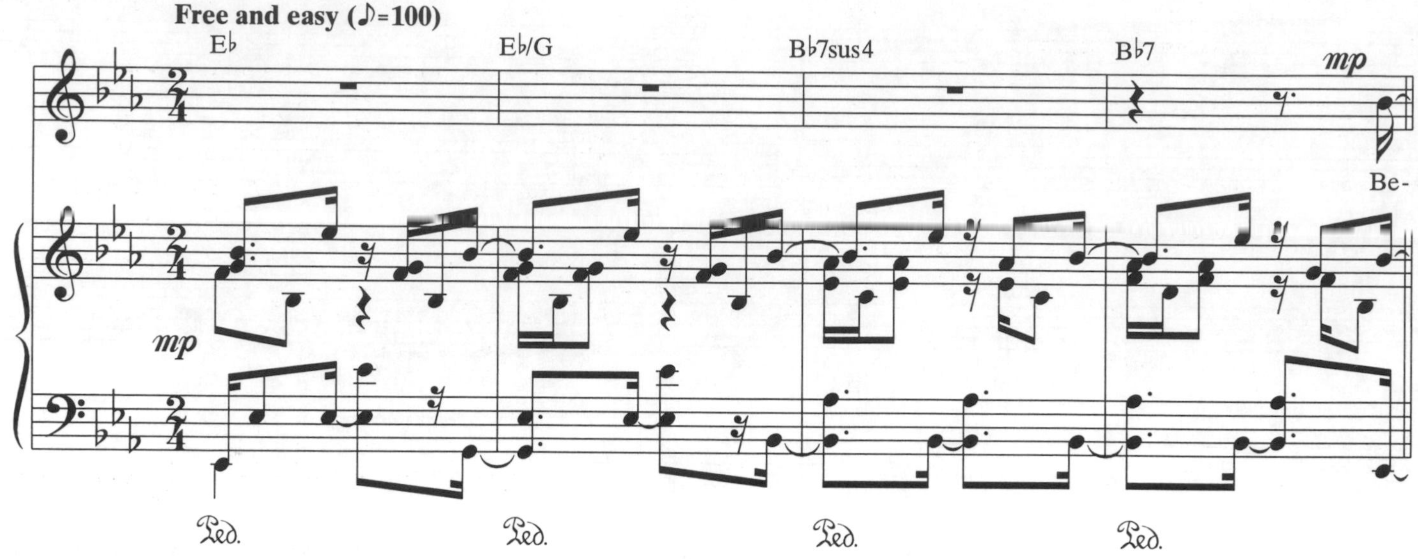

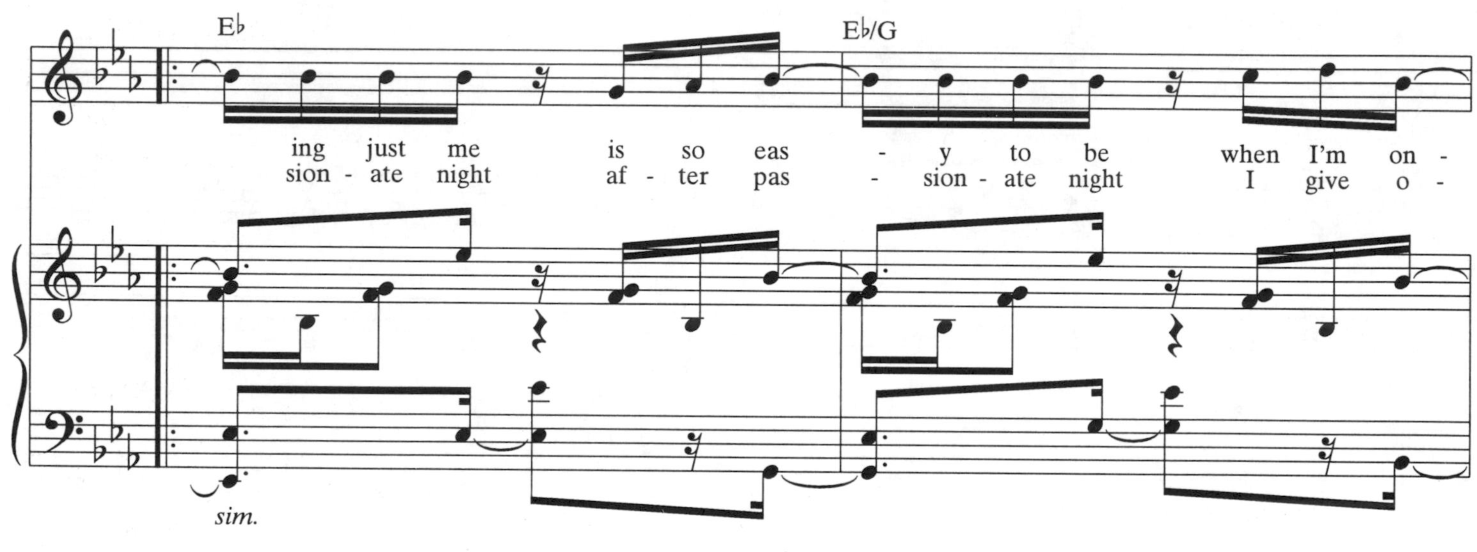

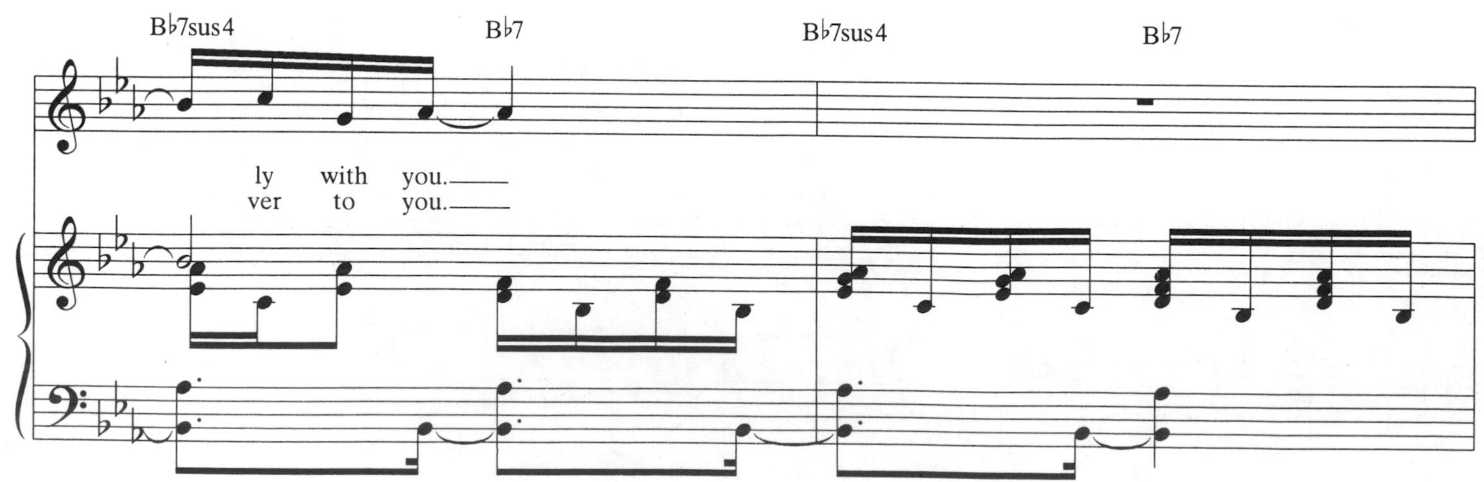

Fm7
B♭7sus4
O - pen in - side and with noth - ing to hide from your view.
Ut - ter - ly changed, I'm at each pre - ar - ranged ren - dez - vous.
Gm7
C7
A♭maj7
Seems long a - go I was des -
Lured by the fire of your end -
Dm7♭5
G7
Cm
Cm/B♭
F7
tined to know, and the mo - ment I saw you I knew,
less de - sire, I still won - der the way that it grew.
E♭/G
A♭
Fm7
B♭7sus4
I could be to - tal - ly hap - py with no - one but
Nev - er e - lu - sive it comes from ex - clu - sive - ly
3

1.
E♭
E♭/G
B♭7sus4
you.
Pas -
2.
E♭
E♭7sus4
E♭7
A♭maj7
you.
Find - ing a spe - cial per -
B♭7sus4
Gm7/C
son we can love is so rare,
C7
F7
how in the world can there

F7/A
B♭7sus4
be two?
E♭
E♭/G
Send me a love that will mend me with love, I am des -
B♭7sus4
B♭7
B♭7sus4
B♭7
Fm7
p'rate for you,
giv - ing you chase like some god -
B♭7sus4
Gm7/C
C7
dess of grace I pur - sue.

A♭maj7
Dm7♭5
G7
Blind - ed by need, I will fol - low your lead mon - key see,
Cm
Cm/B♭
F7
E♭/G
A♭
mon-key say, mon-key do.
Tak - en for grant - ed, com - plete -
Fm7
B♭7sus4
E♭
E♭7sus4
E♭7
ly en - chant - ed by you.
Small
A♭maj7
Dm7♭5
G7
won - der it seems that my life's made of dreams and of wish -

Cm
Cm/B♭
F7
rit.
es that nev - er come true.
I
rit.
E♭/G
A♭
Fm7
Fm7/B♭
a tempo
would-n't be lone - ly if I could be on - ly
a tempo
rit.
a tempo
E♭
E♭/G
with you,
with
Show lyric: and
rit.
a tempo
A♭maj7
B♭7sus4
rit.
E♭
you,
and
you.
you,
and
you.
rit.

from VICTOR/VICTORIA

Paris By Night

Words by Leslie Bricusse
Music by Henry Mancini

G7/C
Cm6
F7
B♭7
E♭
B♭7
E♭
bars of Les Halles, the bras-s'ries and the ca - fés of Mont - par - nasse. The
Fm7
B♭7
E♭maj7
Fm/A♭
cab - a - rets and bis - tros where the writ - er or ar - tiste goes are as
Dm7♭5
G7
Cm
Fm7
B♭7
much a part of Par - is as La Tour Eif - fel! The res - t'rants for the pur - ists, the
E♭maj7
Fm/A♭
Am7♭5
D7
A♭7
G7♯5
night - clubs for the tour - ists, we have those in a - bun - dance as well!

Cm6
G7♭9/C
Cm6
A♭7/E♭
Par - ee can be a dan - ger - ous af - fair. She of - fers far more fol - lies than the
Dm7♭5
G7sus4 G7
Cm6
G7♭9/C
Fo - lies Ber - gères! For sheer so - phis - ti - ca - tion, plus some high - er ed - u - ca - tion, the
Fm7/A♭
G7
Cm Gm7♭5/C Cm9
C
Fm7
B♭7
E♭maj7 A♭maj7
smart - er set can't wait to step this way. For here at club "Chez Lui," as you're
F7sus4
F7
A♭7♭5
G7
Dm7add4
G7sus4
G7
all a - bout to see, we'll tell you straight why Gay Par - ee is

Medium cut time
Gm7add4
Gm7/C
C13
B♭/C
gay.
mf
Fmaj7 F6 Fmaj7 E7 F6 Fmaj7 E7 Emaj7
Par - is by night, Par - ee la nuit, se -
E♭maj9 E♭6 E♭maj7 E♭6 D7sus4 D7 D7sus4 D7 Dmaj7
duc - es us in ways we don't ex - pect to be. She has
D♭maj9 Dm7 G7
mag - ic from which ev'n a Hou - di - ni can't be
3

C
Eb9
Eb13
Db/Eb
free.
'Cause
Abmaj7 Ab6
Abmaj7
G7
Ab6
Abmaj7
G7
Gmaj7
Par - is by night has mys - ter - y
that's
Gbmaj7 Gb6
Gbmaj7
Gb6
F7sus4
F7
F7sus4
F7
Fmaj7
haunt - ed us and taunt - ed us through his - to - ry.
Shad - y
Emaj7
C#m/E
Fm7
se - crets
she is all too a -

B♭7 B♭7♭9 E♭
ware we long to share.
B♭m9/E♭ E♭9 E♭7♭9 A♭add2 A♭6
That's why it is, I guess, we
A♭maj9 A♭6 A♭°7 A♭add2
all a - dore her and hun - ger to ex -
A♭6/9 A♭6 G7sus4/D G7
plore her hid - den charms. She

C6/9
Cmaj9
C6
C°7
fools us all be - cause she's so ca - pri - cious, but
Cadd2
C6
Gm7
noth - ing's more de - li - cious than to sleep in her
C7
Gm7
C13
B♭/C
Fmaj7
F6
Fmaj7
E7
arms.
For Par - is by night's the
But Par - is by night you
Fmaj7
F6
Fmaj7
E7
Emaj7
E♭maj7
E♭6
E♭maj7
E♭6
on - ly way to re - al - ize that all in all it's
can't con - demn; they say she's real - ly at her best from

To Coda
D7♭9
D7
Gm7
C♭/D♭
B♭maj9/C
C13♭9
night - time, not the day that sets her a - part,
two to six a. m! C'est vrai, she's sub -
Am11
D13♭9
Gm7
C9
Em7
A9
wins ev - 'ry heart, and makes all our dreams take flight.
Am7
D7
Gm9
B♭maj7/C
There's no dream you can't find in Par - is, Par - ee by
D.S. al Coda
G♭maj9
G♭6
G♭maj9
F7
G♭maj9
G♭6
B♭m7
E♭7
B♭m7
E♭9/G
night.

Coda
C13♭9
Gm7
C9
Am11
D13♭9
lime.
Night-time's the time
Am7♭5
D7♭9
Gm7
C9
Gm/A
A7♭9
when all of our dreams take flight.
D7
D9
D7♭9
Gm7
Gm7/C
B♭/C
There's no dream you can't find in Par-is, Par-ee by
Fmaj9
F6
C♭maj7/D♭
D♭9
F6/9
Fmaj7
night!

from VICTOR/VICTORIA

Paris Makes Me Horny

Words by Leslie Bricusse
Music by Henry Mancini

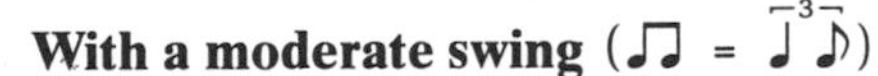

With a moderate swing

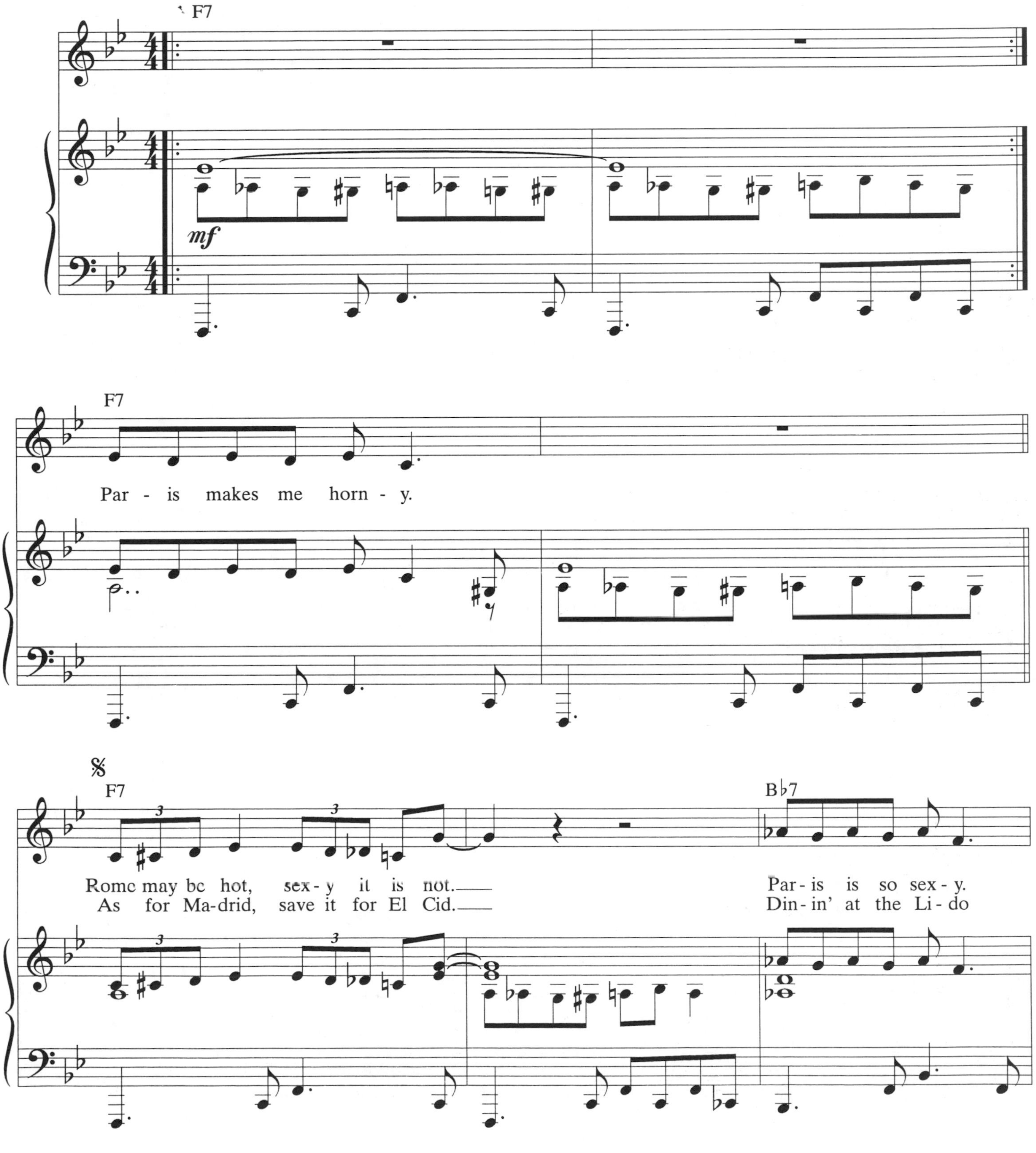

F7

F7

Par - is makes me horn - y.

F7 | B♭7

Rome may be hot, sex - y it is not. Par - is is so sex - y.
As for Ma - drid, save it for El Cid. Din - in' at the Li - do

Fm9/13
F7
Rid-in' in a tax-i gives me ap-o-plex-y.
loos-ens my li-bi-do like a big tor-pe-do.
G7
C9
Been ta Lis-bon, an' Lis-bon is a has-been. Schlepped ta Stock-holm, an'
Seen Ge-ne-va, it's hard-ly jun-gle fe-ver. Been ta Brus-sels, could
A♭7
To Coda
brought a lot-ta schlock home. Al-so Os-lo, an' Os-lo real-ly was slow.
use some red cor-pus-cles. Tried To-ron-to, de-part-ed mol-to pron-to.
F7
Par-is makes me horn-y; it's not like Cal-i-for-ny.

B♭9
Par - is is so diz - zy; Jack, it's such an aph - ro - di - si - ac! Ooh!
It's true.
E♭9
Par - is
thrills me.
D7
When I see the Eif - fel Tower, I have to go and take a shower. It's
true,
I do.
C/E
F6
F♯7♯9
G9
Par - is

D.S. al Coda
C7
B♭/D
E♭m(maj7)
Em7♭5
F6(♯9)
F7
kills me,
and it makes me sex - y.
Coda
F7
F♯7
Par - is makes me tin - gle;
makes me glad I'm sin - gle.
F♯7
B7
Lon - don's o - kay, if it's for one day.
Par - is gets me sex - y
F♯7
in the so - lar plex - y.

G♯9
D7♭5
Been ta Mu-nich where ev-'ry guy's a eu-nuch.
C♯7
D9
C♯7
A7
An' ta Dub-lin, things ain't ex-act-ly bub-blin'. Hate Hel-sin-ki, the
D♯7
F♯7
Finns are kind-a kink-y! But Par-is,
Par-is,
Par-is makes me... ooh, Pooky!
rit.

from FUNNY GIRL

People

Words by Bob Merrill
Music by Jule Styne

need - ing oth - er chil - dren, and yet,
B♭m C7 Fmaj7 F6 G B♭m6 B♭dim7
let - ting our grown - up pride Hide all the need in -
F/A A♭dim7 Gm7 C7
side, act - ing more like chil - dren than
E/F F7 Cm7 F9 B♭
chil - dren. Lov - ers
rit.
a tempo

F7
B♭
Cm7/F
— are ver - y spe - cial peo - ple, they're the
B♭maj7
Fm7
3
luck - i - est peo - ple in the world.
B♭9
E♭
3fr
E♭m
— With one per - son, one ver - y spe - cial
B♭/D
Fm7/B♭
E♭
per - son a feel - ing deep in your soul

F/E♭
B♭/D
Em7♭5
B♭6/D
Gm7
says: you were half, now you're whole.
No more hun - ger and thirst, but
Cm7
F7
B♭
B♭13
first, be a per - son who needs peo - ple.
Peo - ple who need
mf
molto espressivo
E♭
E♭m/G♭
B♭/F
E♭/F
peo - ple are the luck - i - est peo - ple in the
B♭
Gm7
Cm7
F7
world.
decresc.
B♭
Gm7
B♭6
world.
rit.
decresc.
mp

from BYE BYE BIRDIE

Put On A Happy Face

Lyrics by Lee Adams
Music by Charles Strouse

G7
C7
F7
B♭7
E♭maj7
E♭7
E♭6
mask of trag - e - dy, it's not your style;
A♭maj7
D7
G7
C7
F7
Fm7
You'll look so good that you'll be glad ya' de - cid - ed to smile!
B♭9
E♭
E♭6
Gm7
C7
Pick out a pleas - ant out - look,
Fm7
B♭9
Fm7
B♭9
E♭
E♭6
stick out that no - ble chin; Wipe off that "full of

Gm7
C7
Fm7
B♭9
B♭m7
E♭7
doubt" look,
slap on a hap - py grin! And
A♭maj7
B♭9
E♭
3fr
Fm7
B♭7
spread sun - shine all o - ver the
G7+
G7
C9
F9
Fm7
B♭9
place, just put on a hap - py
1
E♭
3fr
E♭6
Fm7
B♭7
2
E♭
3fr
E♭6
Fm7
E♭
3fr
face!
face!

from NINE

Simple

Words and Music by Maury Yeston

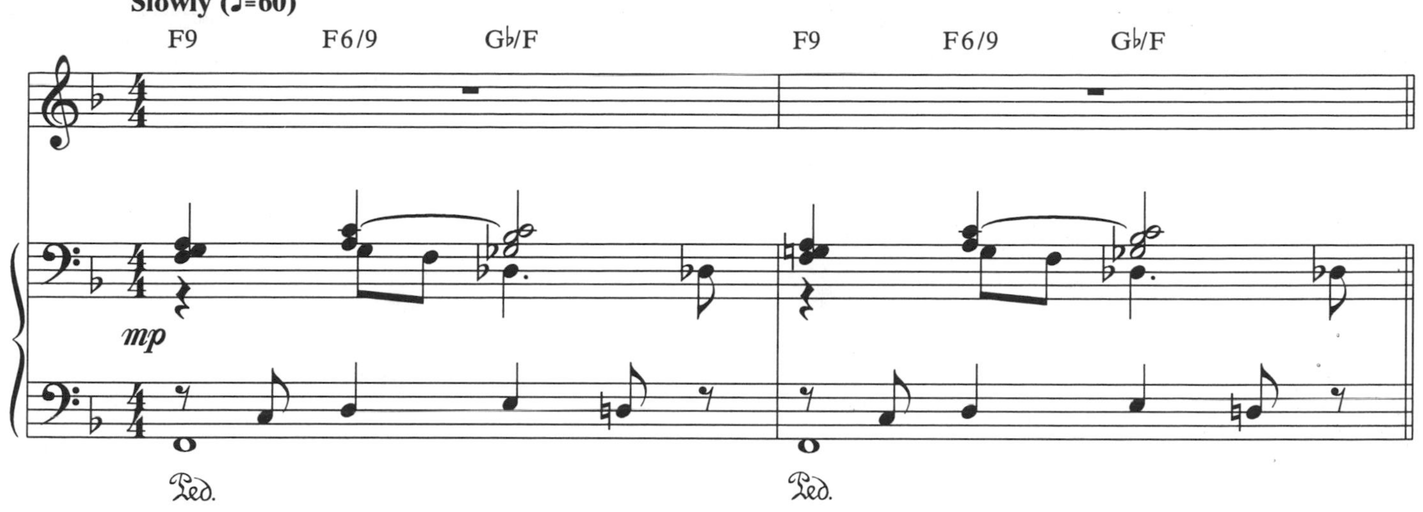

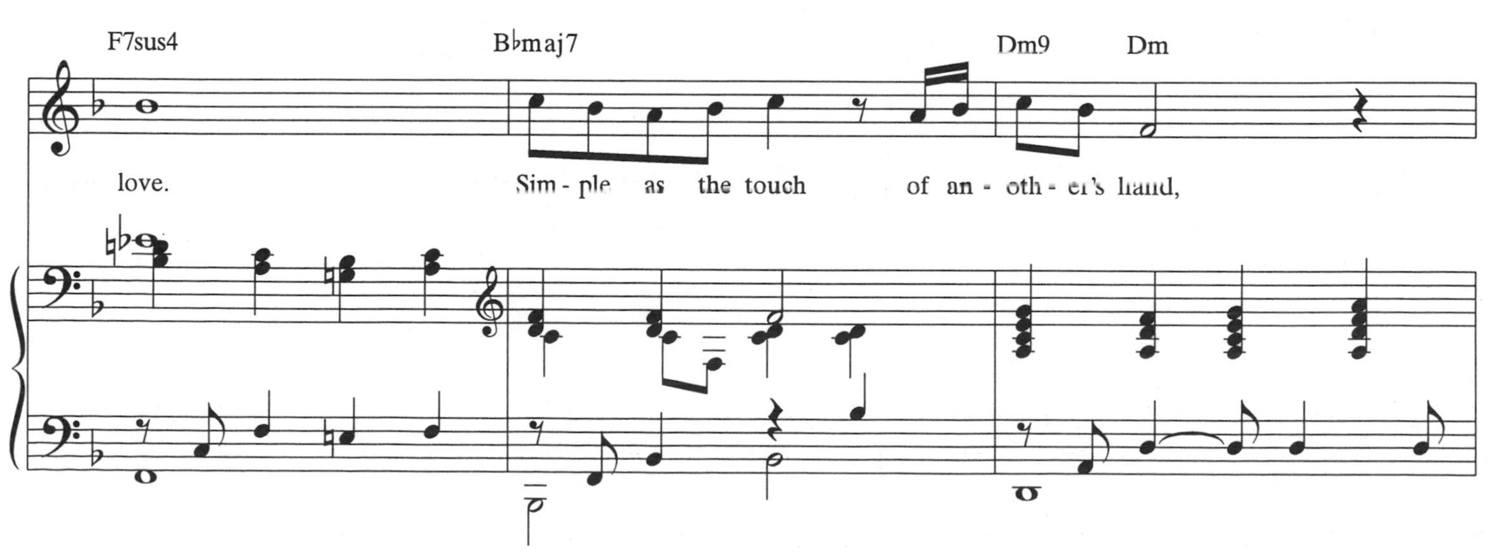

Gm7
C7sus4
sim - ple e - nough for an - y - one to un - der - stand, but
F9 F6/9 G♭/F
you.
Sim - ple are the ways we
come a - part
sim - ple as a babe is new!
F7sus4 F7
B♭maj7
Sim - ple as a tree, and as sim - ple as a cloud, it's as
C7sus4 C7

Am7
D7sus4
D7♭5
D7
sim - ple as the sim - plest things have al - ways been
B♭add2
Gm7
C7sus4
sim - ple as the sun and the moon and the stars in the
A7sus4
A7♭5
A7
A7♯5
A7
Gm7
sky...
Sim - ple are the ways we
C7sus4
C7
F9
F6/9
G♭/F
F9
F6/9
G♭/F
F
say, "Good - bye."

from Meredith Willson's THE MUSIC MAN

Seventy Six Trombones

By Meredith Willson

C7 F D7 G
rows of the fin- est vir- tu- o- sos, The cream of
bong on a Chi- - nese - gong, By a big bang
D7 G D7 G7 C
ev- 'ry fa- mous band. Sev- en- ty Six Trom-
bong- er at the rear. Sev- en- ty Six Trom-
Ebdim G7
bones caught the morn- ing sun, With a hun- dred and
bones hit the count- er- point, While a hun- dred and
C
ten cor- nets right be- hind. There were more than a
ten cor- nets played the air. Then I mod- est- ly
C7 To Coda F D7
thou- sand reeds spring- ing up like weeds, There were
took my place as the

G7
C
horns of ev- 'ry shape and kind. There were
F
B♭
F
F♯dim
C7
cop- per bot- tom tym- pa- ni in horse pla- toons,
fif- ty mount- ed can- non in the bat- ter- y,
E7
Thun- der- ing, thun- der- ing.
Thun- der- ing, thun- der- ing,
sf
F
C7
F
all a- long the way. Dou- ble bell eu-
loud- er than be- fore. Clar- i- nets of
mf
B♭
F
1. C
G7
phon- i- ums and big bas- soons, Each bas- soon
ev- 'ry size and

C
G7
C7
f
mf
2. Bb
having his big fat say. There were trumpeters who'd
E7
F
C7
F
improvise a full octave higher than the score.
G7
D.S. al Coda
Seventy
D.S. al Coda
CODA
F
D7
one and only bass, And I
C
G
C
oompahed, oompahed, oompahpahed
G
G7
C7
oompahed up and down the square.

from JEKYLL & HYDE

Someone Like You

Words by Leslie Bricusse
Music by Frank Wildhorn

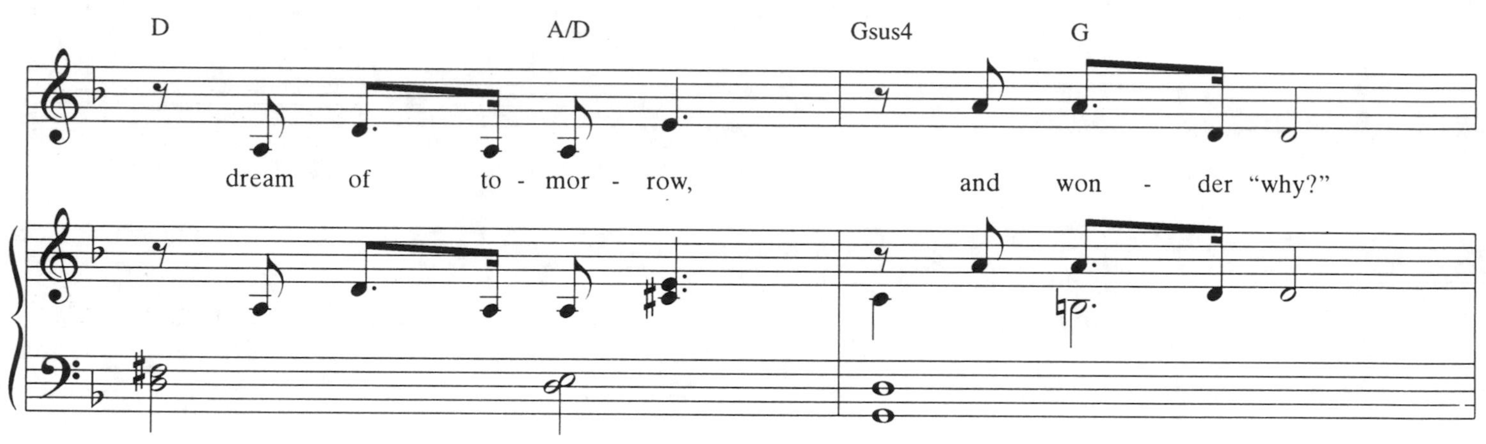

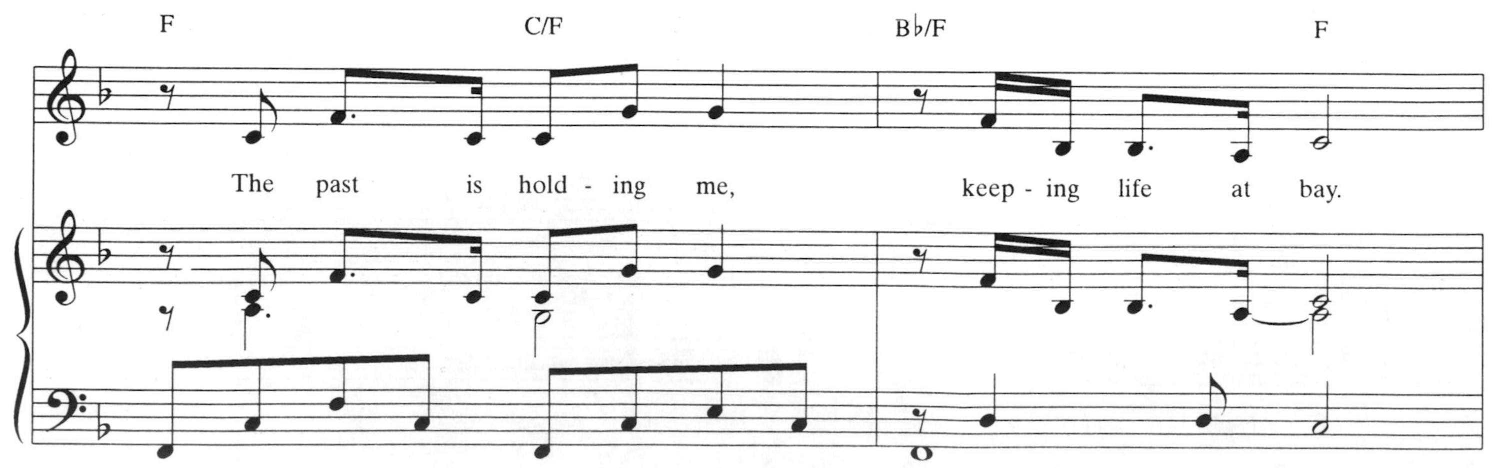

C/F
A/C♯
Dm
Dm/C
I wan - der, lost in yes - ter - day, want - ing to
B♭
Gm7
B♭/C
F
fly, but scared to try. But if some - one like you found
Gm7
Fsus4
F/A
some - one like me, then sud - den - ly noth - ing would
B♭
Gm7♭5
F
Gm
ev - er be the same! My heart would take wing and I'd

F/A
Gm7
F
Dm7
Gm7
D♭/E♭
feel so a - live, if some - one like you found
rit.
Fadd2
Em7
G/A
Dadd2
A/D
me!
So man - y se - crets
a tempo
mp
Gadd2/D
D
A/D
I long to share!
All I have need - ed
Gsus4
G
F
C/F
is some - one there
to help me see a world

B♭/F
F
Asus4
A
I've nev - er seen be - fore,
a love to o - pen ev - 'ry
Dm
Dm/C
B♭
Gm7
door,
to set me free
so I can
B♭/C
F
soar!
If some - one like you found
cresc.
mf
Gm7
Fsus4
F/A
some - one like me,
then sud - den - ly
noth - ing would

B♭
Gm7♭5
F
Dm
Gm7
ev - er be the same! There'd be a new way to live a
F
Dm
Gm7
F
Dm
Gm7
C7sus4
new life to love, if some - one like you found
D♭maj7
C♭/D♭
G♭
me! Oh, if some - one like you found
cresc.
rit.
f a tempo
A♭m7
G♭sus4
G♭
some - one like me, then sud - den - ly nothing would
3

C♭maj7
A♭m7♭5
G♭
E♭m
A♭m7
ev - er be the same! My heart would take wing, and I'd
B♭m7
D♭/E♭
E♭7
Slower, freely
A♭m7
feel so a - live, if some - one like
rit.
p
D♭sus4
G♭add2
C♭maj7
you loved me, loved
G♭add2
C♭maj7
N.C.
G♭add2
me, loved me!

from TITANIC

Still

Music and Lyrics by Maury Yeston

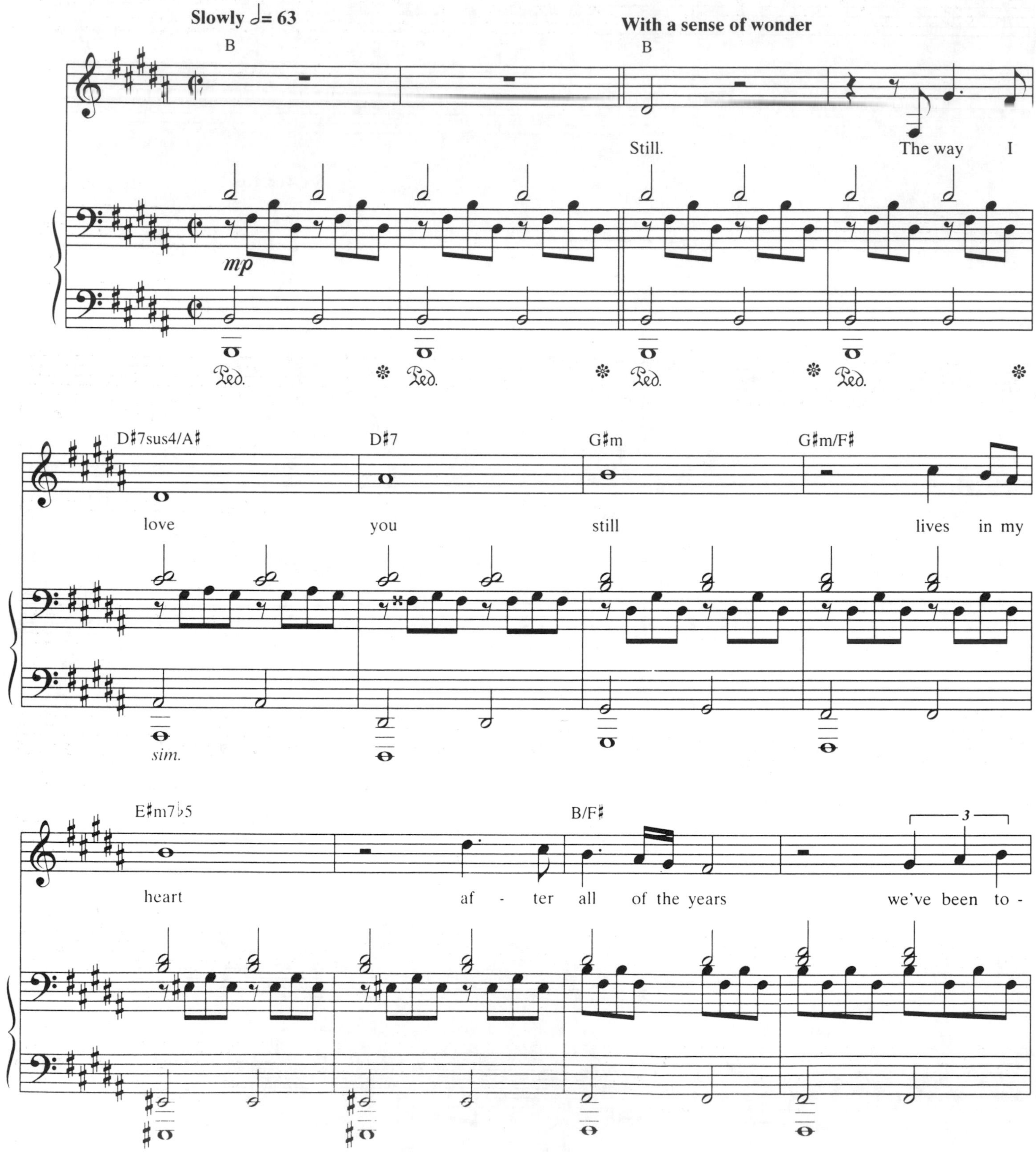

Slowly 𝅗𝅥 = 63

With a sense of wonder

B B

Still. The way I

D♯7sus4/A♯ D♯7 G♯m G♯m/F♯

love you still lives in my

E♯m7♭5 B/F♯

heart af - ter all of the years we've been to -

mp

sim.

E/F♯
F♯7sus4
F♯7
G♯m
F♯/A♯
geth - er hold -
cresc.
B
F♯m/A
G♯7sus4
G♯7
D♯m7♭5
our love still. The way you
mf
G♯7sus4
G♯7
C♯m
C♯m/B
move me still feels as it
cresc.
F♯7/A♯
E♯m7♭5
B/F♯
did when you first be - came mine, whis - pered the
3

E/F♯
F♯7sus4
F♯7
B
C♯7/G♯
words
"I
will."
I
B/F♯
F♯
B/F♯
E/F♯
F♯7sus4
F♯7
loved you then
and I love
you
B
B9sus4
B7
Eadd2
A♯7♯5
A♯7
still.
No one else could
D♯9sus4
D♯m/C♯
Eadd2
A♯7♯5
A♯7
play your role,
for - ev - er know my

D♯m
G♯/D♯
A♯m
G♯/B♯
A♯m/C♯
mind. True com - pan - ion
f
D♯7sus4
D♯
G♯add2
A♯m7♭5
D♯7sus2
D♯7
of my soul I won't turn from,
G♯9sus4
G♯9
G7♯9/D
G♯7/D♯
D♭add2
D♭
you I learn from. Still. Through for - tune's
molto rit.
a tempo
mp
F7sus4/C
F7
B♭madd2
B♭madd2/A♭
chang - es still al - ways we've

Gm7♭5
D♭/A♭
known that the prom - ise we made kept us as
B♭♭/A♭
A♭7sus4
A♭7
D♭
E♭7/B♭
mf
one and will! I
sfz
cresc.
poco rit.
a tempo
mf
*Cue notes are an alternate melody.
D♭/A♭
A♭9sus4
A♭7
loved you - then and I love you
sfz
sfz
molto cresc.
poco rit.
E/D♭
F♯/D♭
D♭
still.
a tempo
ff
rit.

from JEKYLL & HYDE

This Is The Moment

Words by Leslie Bricusse
Music by Frank Wildhorn

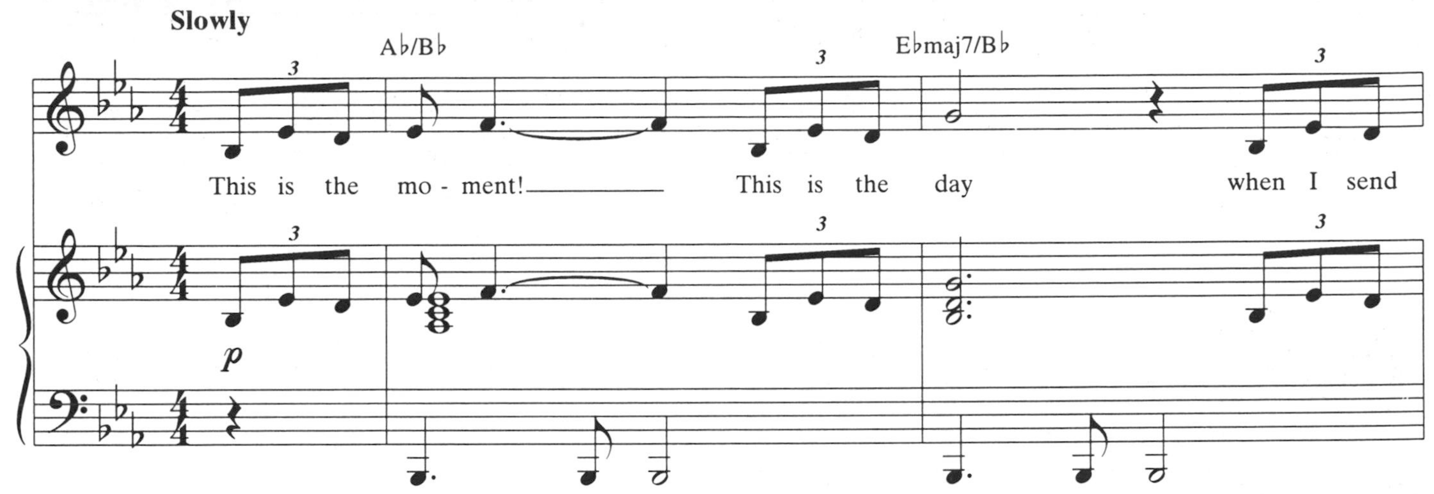

Fm
E♭/G
A♭
coming into play, is here and now today!
B♭sus4
A♭/B♭
This is the moment, this is the
mp
E♭maj7
A♭/B♭
time when the momentum and the moment are in
E♭maj7
Cmadd2
Gm
rhyme! Give me this moment, this precious chance. I'll

Fm
E♭/G
A♭
A♭/B♭
gath - er up my past and make some sense at last! This is the
E♭
Fm/E♭
E♭
Fm7♭5/E♭
mo - ment when all I've done, all of the
mo - ment, my fi - nal test. Des - ti - ny
mf
E♭
Cm
A♭maj7
B♭/A♭
dream - ing, schem - ing and scream - ing be - come one! This is the
beck - oned, I nev - er reck - oned sec - ond best! I won't look
To Coda
Fm
B♭/A♭
Gm
Cm
day, see it spar - kle and shine, when all I've
down, I must not fall! This is the

Fm
Ab/Bb
Eb
Bb/Ab
Ab
Gm7
Eb/G
lived for be - comes mine!
For all these years I've
Bb/Ab
Eb/G
Fm
Eb/G
faced the world a - lone,
and now the time has come to
D.S. al Coda
Abm
Bbsus4
Ab/Bb
prove to them I made it on my own!
This is the
Coda
Fm
Eb/G
Fm
Ab/Bb
Eb
B7
mo - ment, the sweet - est mo - ment of them all!
This is the

E F♯m/E E F♯m7♭5/E E C♯m
mo - ment! Damn all the odds! This day or nev - er, I'll sit for - ev - er with the
Amaj7 B/A F♯m B/A G♯m C♯m
gods! When I look back, I will al - ways re - call moment for
F♯m E/G♯ A E/G♯ F♯m A/B B7
mo - ment, this was the mo - ment, the great - est mo - ment of them
A/E F♯7/E F♯m/E A/B B7 E
all!
rit.

from the Stage Production ANNIE GET YOUR GUN

There's No Business Like Show Business

Words and Music by Irving Berlin

G7 Cmaj7 C C9
hap - py men be - cause the butch - er, the
lifts you when you're down, the head - aches, the
move the show at dawn, the mu - sic, the
F♯dim Fm6 C/E Cm/E♭
bak - er, the gro - cer, the clerk get
heart - aches, the back - aches, the flops the
mu - sic, the spot - light, the towns your
D7 G7 C Dm7/C C
paid for what they do but no ap - plause. They'd
sher - iff who es - corts you out of town. The
bag - gage with the lab - els pas - ted on. The
E E/B F♯m7 B7
glad - ly bid their drear - y jobs good - bye, for
open - ing when your heart beats like a drum, the
saw - dust and the hor - ses and the smell, the

C C/G Dm7 G7
an - y - thing the - a - tri - cal and why. There's
clos - ing when the cus - tom - ers won't come. There's
towel you've tak - en from the last ho - tel. There's
rit.
a tempo
C
no bus - 'ness like show bus - 'ness like
no bus - 'ness like show bus - 'ness like
no bus - 'ness like show bus - 'ness like
Fm/G Cmaj7 C
no bus - 'ness I know.
no bus - 'ness I know.
no bus - 'ness I know.
G7 Dm7 G7 C
Ev - 'ry - thing a - bout it is ap - peal - ing.
You get word be - fore the show has start - ed.
Trav - 'ling thru the coun - try will be thrill - ing.

G7
Dm7
G7
C
Dm7/G
Ev - 'ry - thing the traf - fic will al - low.
That your fav - 'rite un - cle died at dawn.
Stand - ing out in front on open - ing nights.
G7
Dm7
G7
Am
No - where could you get that hap - py feel - ing
Top of that your Pa and Ma have part - ed,
Smil - ing as you watch the thea - tre fill - ing,
Am7
Am7/D
D7
Dm7/G
when you are steal - ing that ex - tra bow.
you're brok - en - heart - ed but you go on.
and there's your bill - ing out there in lights.
G7
C
There's no peo - ple like
There's no peo - ple like
There's no peo - ple like

C7
show peo - ple. They smile when
show peo - ple. They don't run
show peo - ple. They smile when
C7/G
Fmaj7
F6
they are low.
out of dough.
they are low.
Dm7
B♭7♭5
A7
E - ven with a tur - key that you know will fold.
An - gels come from ev - 'ry - where with lots of jack.
Yes - ter - day they told you you would not go far.
A♭7♭5
G7
You may be strand - ed out
And when you lose it, there's
That night you o - pen and

C
A7
Dm7
in the cold.
no at - tack.
there you are.
Still you would - n't
Where could you get
Next day on your
B♭7♭5
A7
change it for a sack of gold.
mon - ey that you don't give back.
dress - ing room they've hung a star.
Let's
A♭7♭5
G7
1,2
C
Em
go on with the show.
Dm7
G7
3
C
Dm/G
C
There's
show.

from PHANTOM

This Place Is Mine

Words and Music by Maury Yeston

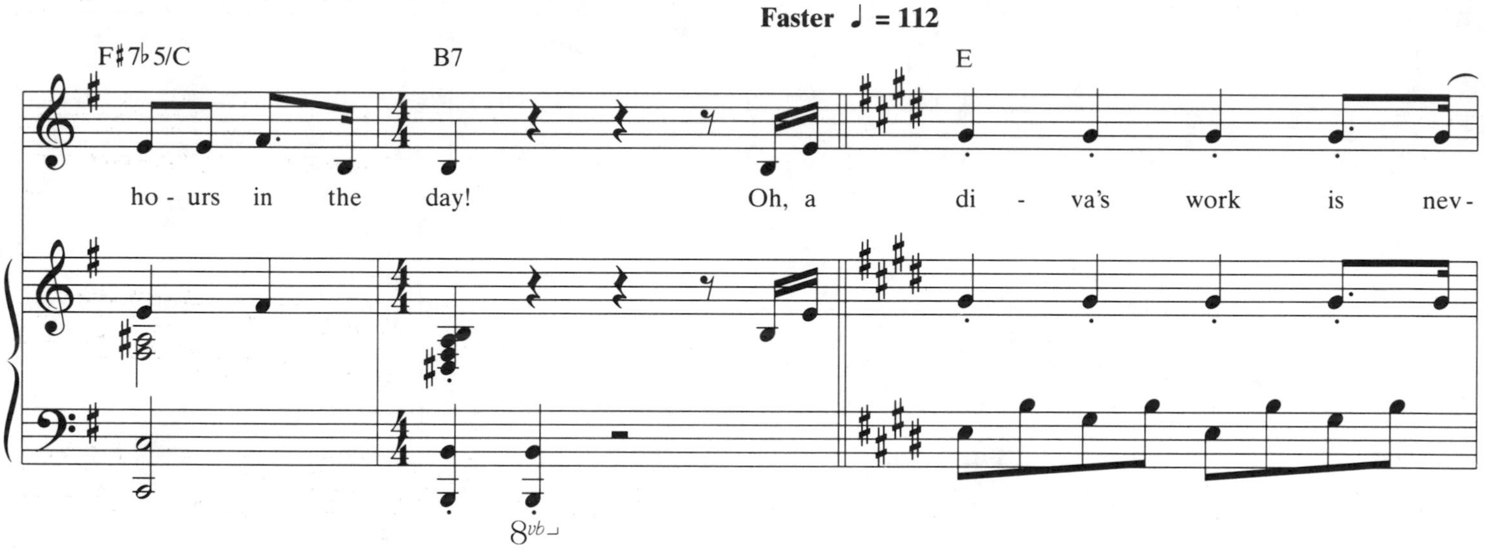

E
B7/D♯
C♯m/E
F♯7/A♯
if the di - va has___ to run an___ op - 'ra com - pa -
B
Em
B7/D♯
ny. Ev-'ry small de - tail to su - per-vise, ev-'ry
8vb
C/E
F♯7/A♯
B7
pret - ty face to___ scru - ti -
Em
B7/D♯
C/E
F♯7/A♯
nize. I plan be - neath these eyes this___ op - 'ra com - pa -
3

B7
Am/E
F♯m7♭5/E
Em
ny.
Why take on this ar - duous chore?
8vb
F♯m7♭5/E
A°7/E
Em
Sleep - less nights I pace___ a - cross my bed - room floor; why
Am/E
F♯m7♭5/E
Em
do I live com - plete - ly for this
C
F♯7♭5/A♯
B7
op - - 'ra com - pa - ny? 'Cause it's
rit.

Intensely ♩ = 88
Em
Em(maj7)
mine, from the stalls to the por - traits on the walls, to the
sing, I will glow, I will nev - er let it go, I will
mf
Em7
A/E
A°7/E
bal - con - ies and log - es far and near. It be - longs all to me, ev - 'ry
hold it ev - er cap - tive in my hand. Like a god, like a queen, I will
i - tem that you see, from the cel - lar to the crys - tal chan - de -
en - ter an - y scene, and con - trol it like a king - dom I com -
Em9
E7
Am
lier. From the flut - ed mar - ble grand fa - cade, to the
mand. And I pit - y an - y bar - i - tone who at -

F♯°7/B
Gmaj7
Cmaj7
el - e - vat - ed prom - e-nade, From ev - 'ry
tempts to tread the stage I own. With no po -
F♯m7♭5
C7♭5
B7sus4
toil - et bowl, to ev - 'ry lead - ing role,
lite re-quest, he's here at my be-hest,
1.
B7♭5
Emadd2
A°7/E
this place is mine! I will
'cause it's all
2.
Emadd2
Em6
Am7
mine! My cur - tain

C/D
C/G
Bm/C
and my can - o - py, my
F♯m7♭5
F♯7♭5/C
B
B/E
Em
song, my key, my chart.
B7/E
Em
Am7
C/D
My grand ro - man - tic
C/G
Bm/C
F♯m7♭5
des - ti - ny, from here my

C7
B7sus4
B7
life will start. I'll be
Em
Em(maj7)
out on the stage look - ing great and half my age, ev - 'ry
Em7
A/E
chance I get I'll get 'em on their feet. I will
A°7/E
burn, I will scheme, I will re - al - ize my dream, 'cause if

Em9
I'm not in a light I'm in - com - plete. And the
E7
Am
F♯°7/B
best part I'm just coming to, how they'll all ap - plaud for
Gmaj7
Cmaj7
F♯m7♭5
you know who. I can't be - lieve I'm here,
F♯7♭5/C
B7sus4
B7
Am/B
and this is my ca - reer! It
ff

Em/C♯
D♯m(♭5)
Em
Em(maj7)
must be seen like a torch, we'll en - grave it on the porch! Like an
Em7
F♯m7♭5/E
e - dict, like a bea - con, like a sign.
This
B7sus4
B7♭5
place
is
Emadd2
A°7/E
Em
mine!
8vb

from THE PRODUCERS

'Til Him

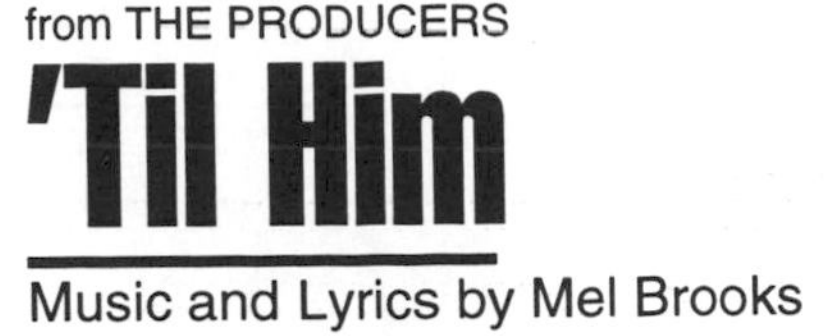

Music and Lyrics by Mel Brooks

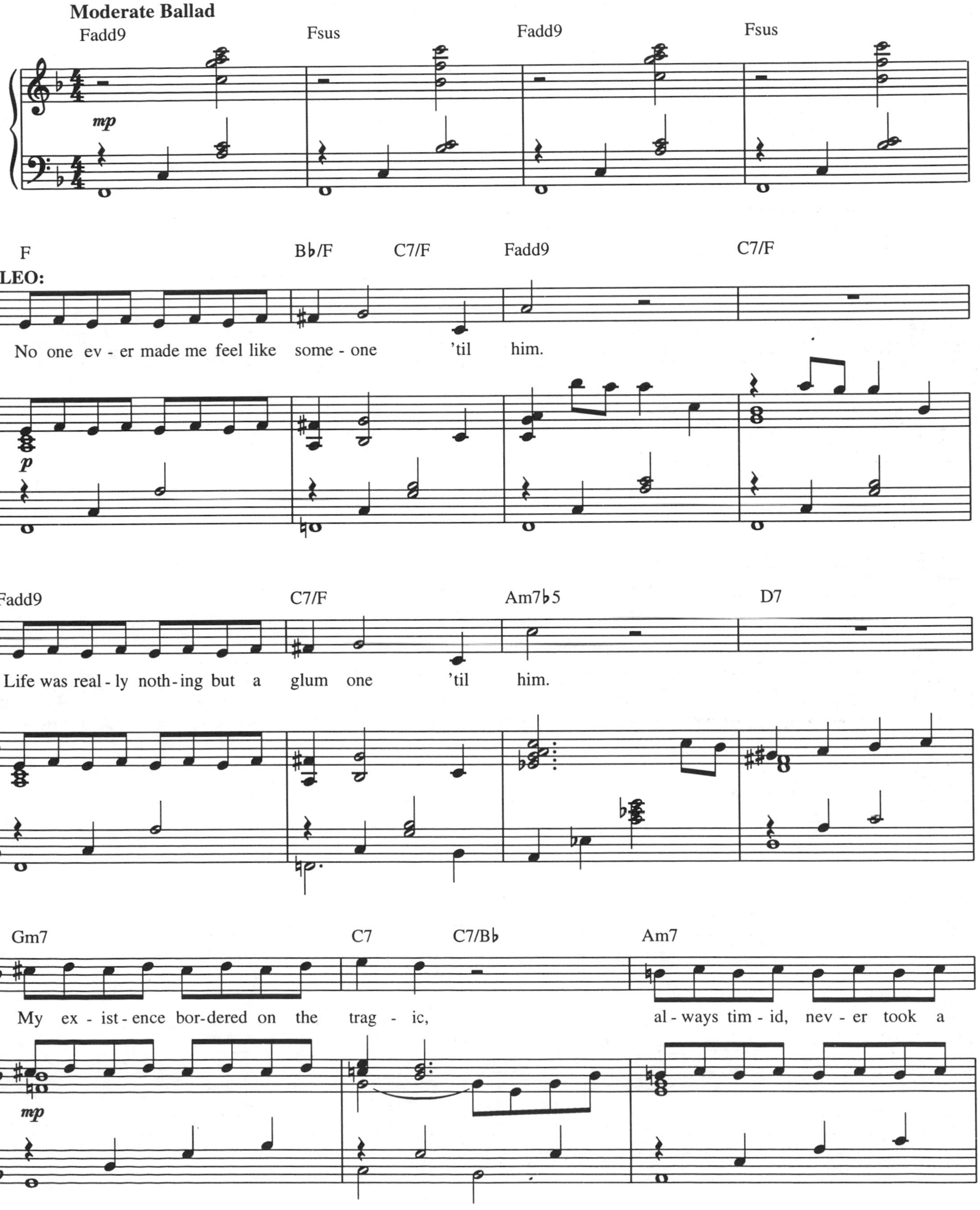
Moderate Ballad
Fadd9 Fsus Fadd9 Fsus
mp
F Bb/F C7/F Fadd9 C7/F
LEO:
No one ever made me feel like someone 'til him.
p
Fadd9 C7/F Am7b5 D7
Life was really nothing but a glum one 'til him.
Gm7 C7 C7/Bb Am7
My existence bordered on the tragic, always timid, never took a
mp

D7
Gm
Cdim7/G
G7sus
G7
C7
chance,
then I felt his mag - ic
and my heart be - gan
to
dance!
Gm7/C
C13
F
B♭/F
C7
Fmaj7
I was al - ways frigh - tened, fraught with
wor - ry
'til
him.
mp
C7/F
Fadd9
C7/F
Am7♭5
I was go - ing no - where in a
hur - ry
'til
him.
D7
B♭
Gm7♭5
He
filled up
my
emp - ty life,
f

Am7
Am7/D
D7
G7sus
G7
B♭/C
Gm7♭5/C
filled it to the brim.
There could nev - er ev - er be an - oth - er one like
poco rit.
a tempo
mp
poco rit.
F
C7
F
F♯m7/B
him.
B9
E
A/E
B7/E
MAX:
No one ev - er ev - er real - ly knew me 'til
mp
Eadd9
A/E
B7
E
B7/E
B7/A
him.
Ev - 'ry - one was al - ways out to screw me 'til

G#m7♭5
C#7♭5
C#7
F#m7
him.
Nev - er met a man I ev - er
B7
G#m7
C#9
trust - ed,
al - ways dealt with shy - sters in the past.
F#m7
Fdim7
F#7sus
F#
B7sus
Now I'm well - ad - just - ed 'cause I've got a friend at last.
poco rit.
poco rall.
B9
C9
A Tempo
Fmaj7
B♭/F
C7/F
Al - ways play - ing sin - gles, nev - er dou - bles 'til
mp

F
Bb/F
Fadd9
C7/F
him.
Nev - er had a pal to share my trou - bles 'til
Am7b5
D7
LEO & MAX:
Gm7
Bbm
him.
He filled up my emp - ty life
f
Am7
Am7/D
D7
LEO:
G7sus
G7
Gm7b5
Filled it to the brim
There could nev - er ev - er be an - oth - er one
poco rit.
poco rit.
Slowly
F
Bb/F
Fadd9
like him.

from THOROUGHLY MODERN MILLIE

Thoroughly Modern Millie

Words by Sammy Cahn
Music by James Van Heusen

F/C
G7
C7
heav - en knows, the world has gone to rack and to
F6
F°7
F6
F°7
ruin.
F6
F°7
F6
A7
What we
f
mf
Dm
Dm(maj7)
Dm7
think is chic, u - nique, and quite a - dor - a - ble,

G9
F6/C
D♭7♭5
they think is odd ___ and Sod - om and ___ Go -
cresc.
C
D♭/C
B♭7♭5
mor - rah - ble! ___
f
A7 Tacet
D
But the fact is ev - 'ry - thing to - day is thor - ough - ly
mf
E9
E13
Tacet
A7
A7/B
mod - ern. ___ (Check your per - son - al - i - ty.) Ev - 'ry - thing to -

C°7
A7/C♯
D7
D9
Tacet
day makes yes - ter - day slow.
(Bet - ter face re - al - i - ty.)
G
Gm6
D
F♯7/C♯
It's not in - san - i - ty, says *Van - i - ty*
Bm
E13
F♯m
G°
E7/G♯
Fair. In fact, it's styl - ish to
N.C.
A7
A°7
A7
A°7
raise your skirts and bob your hair,
Raise your skirts and bob your hair,
Raise your skirts and

F9 E9 A7
D6
bob your hair!
bob your hair!
Have you seen the way they kiss in the
E9 E13 N.C.
A7
mov - ies?
(Is - n't it de - lect - a - ble?)
Paint - ing lips and
N.C. F♯13
Tacet
pen - cil - lin - ing your brow
now is quite re - spect - a - ble.
G
Gm6
D
Good - bye,
good good - y girl,
I'm chang - ing, and

B9
Em7
A
Em7
A7
Em7
A7
Em7
how.
So
beat
the
drums 'cause
here
comes Thor - ough - ly
Mod - ern
G/A
A7
D6
B♭7
D
B°7
Mil - lie
now!
F♯7
Bm
Bm(maj7)
What
we
think
is
chic,
u - nique,
and
quite
a -
Bm7
E9
Bm
dor - a - ble,
they
think
is
odd
and

E7
A
Sod - om and Go - mor - rah - ble! But the fact is,
F Tacet
G9
ev - 'ry - thing to - day is thor - ough - ly mod - ern.
mp
Tacet
C7
(Bands are get - tin' jazz - i - er.) Ev - 'ry - thing to - day is start - ing to
Tacet
F13
Tacet
B6
go. (Cars are get - tin' snaz - zi - er.) Men say
mf

B♭m
F/C
A7
Dm
it's crim - i - nal what wom - en - 'll do.
G9
N.C.
C7
What they're for - get - ting is this is nine - teen
twen - ty - two!
F
f
G7
Am7
B♭m6
G7/B
C9

F9
B♭6
Good - bye,
B♭m
good good -
y girl,
F/C
I'm chang - ing, and
D9
how!
mf cresc.
Tacet
I'm chang - ing, and
f
A7
D9
how!
So
mp

N.C.
beat the drums 'cause here comes thor - ough - ly Hot off the press! One step
grad. cresc.
a - head! Jazz Age! Whoop - ee, ba - by! We're so Thor - ough - ly
Gm7
Tacet
Mod - ern Mil - lie
f
R.H.
gliss.
F
D♭7
F6
now!
ff
gliss.
gliss.

from JEKYLL & HYDE

Till You Came Into My Life

Words by Leslie Bricusse
Music by Frank Wildhorn

F#
Badd2
4 fr.
me, in my world safe where no one's ever
er. In your eyes there's excitement, there is
A/B
F#
C#m7
4 fr.
found me. Never knowing what could
wonder. Like a ship adrift at
B/D#
4 fr.
E
B/F#
F#
be, what was there inside of me; I never let those feelings in.
sea, I had wandered endlessly, searching for a shelter.
C#m7
4 fr.
B/D#
4 fr.
E
Then upon a summer's night, you gently changed my life. I would never
Like a sweet imagined dream, you were heaven-sent to me; you gave my heart a

B/F♯
F♯
B
B
be the— same.—
home.
Till you came in - to my life,
mf
D♯m7
6 fr.
G♯m7
4 fr.
C♯m7
4 fr.
F♯
till I heard you call my name,———
I was liv - ing in a
To Coda
C♯m
4 fr.
C♯m/B
Amaj7
F♯sus4
F♯
B
world of grey, each day just like the one be - fore.
You have giv - en me my
D♯m7
6 fr.
G♯m7
4 fr.
C♯m7
4 fr.
eyes,
you have taught me how to see.———

F♯
C♯m
4 fr.
C♯m/B
Amaj7
And now I see a brand - new world I nev - er dreamed could
F♯sus4
E/F♯
Bsus4
2 fr.
be, till you came in - to my life.
p
E/B
F♯/B
Bsus4
2 fr.
D.S. al Coda
Coda
F♯7sus4
B
G♯m
4 fr.
Till you came in - to my life.
With - out the stars the night is
sempre staccato

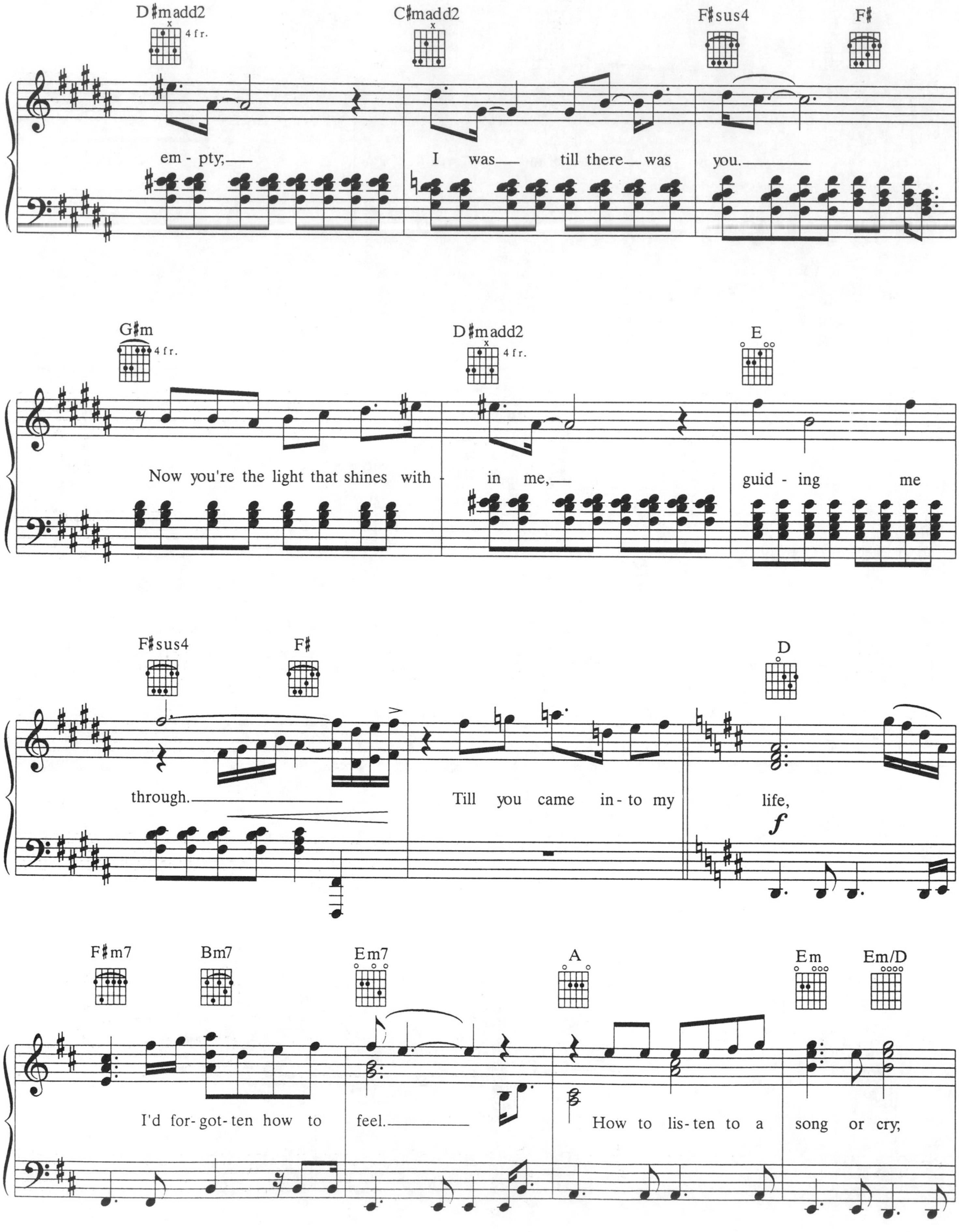
D♯madd2
4 fr.
C♯madd2
F♯sus4
F♯
em - pty,
I was
till there
was
you.
G♯m
4 fr.
D♯madd2
4 fr.
E
Now you're the light that shines with -
in me,
guid - ing
me
F♯sus4
F♯
D
through.
Till you came in - to my
life,
f
F♯m7
Bm7
Em7
A
Em
Em/D
I'd for - got - ten how to
feel.
How to lis - ten to a
song or cry;

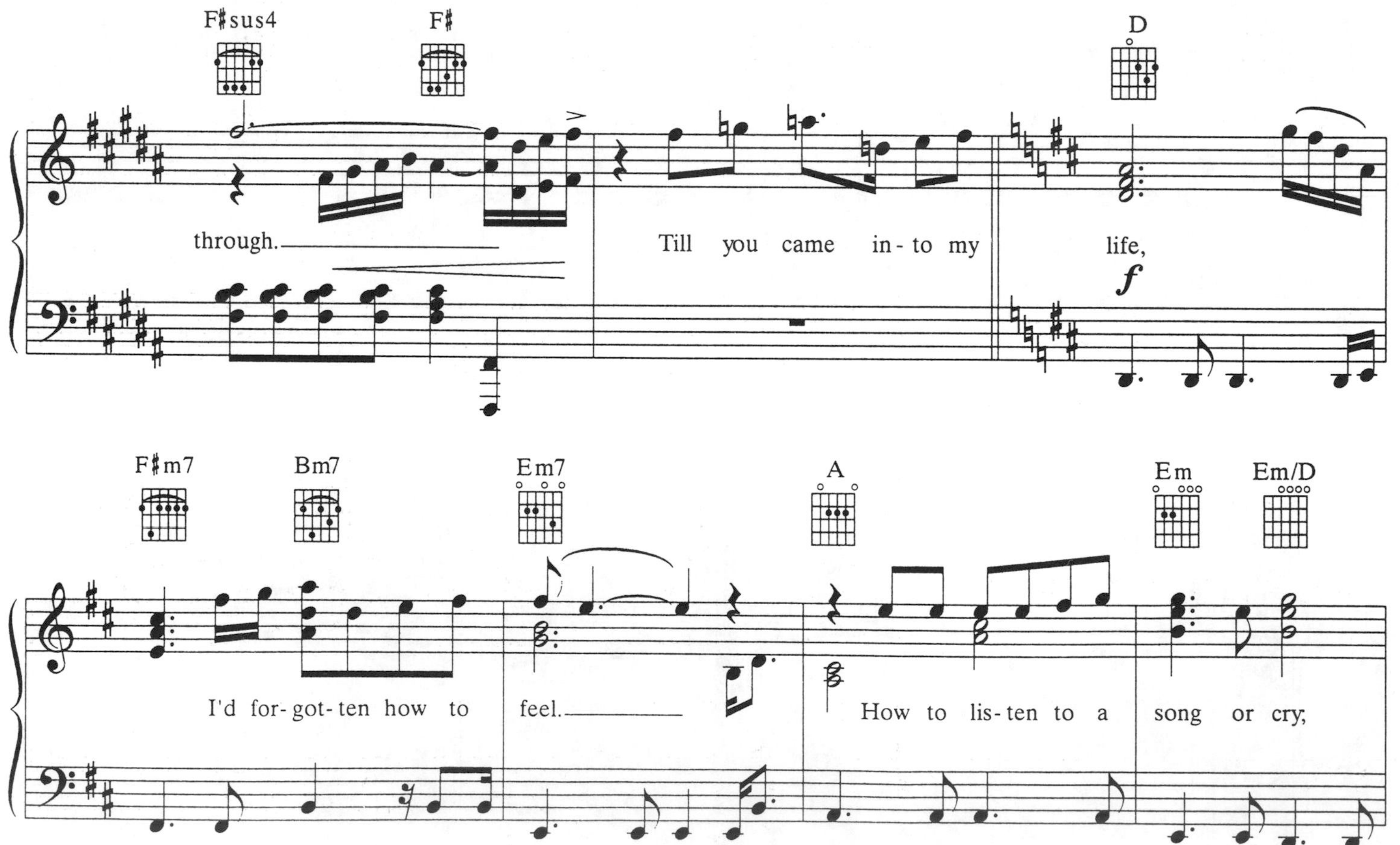

Cmaj7
Asus4
A
D
I'd lost the child in me.
Till you came in-to my
F♯m7
Bm7
Em7
life,
I had nev-er want-ed more.
A
Em
Em/D
Cmaj7
Asus4
Then you said you need-ed me, and sud-den-ly my heart could soar.
A
D
Bm7
G
Em7/A
D
For-ev-er stay with me.
rit.

from the Musical Production ANNIE

Tomorrow

Lyrics by Martin Charnin
Music by Charles Strouse

B♭maj7
Am7
Dm
Dm/C
clears a - way the cob - webs and the sor - row till there's
B♭maj7
C
Fm
A♭/E♭
none. When I'm stuck with a day that's gray and
D♭
E♭
3fr
A♭
4fr
A♭maj7
lone - ly, I just stick out my chin and grin and
C7sus
C7
say: Oh! the
f
mp

F
Fmaj7
B♭maj7
Am7
sun - 'll come out to - mor - row,
So you
Oh! I
got to hang on till to -
Dm
Dm/C
G♭maj7
C7sus
C7
mor - row come what may! To -
1 (small notes are optional harmony)
F
Fmaj7
F7
B♭
B♭m6
6fr
mor - row, to - mor - row, I love ya to - mor - row, you're
F
C7sus
C7
F
Fmaj7
B♭maj7/F
Gm7(add4)
al - ways
on - ly
a day a - way!
The

2
F
Fmaj7
F7
B♭
B♭m6
6fr
mor - row, to - mor - row, I love ya to - mor - row, you're
C7sus
C7
{al - ways / on - ly} a day a - way! To - mor - row, to - mor - row, I
love ya to - mor - row, you're {al - ways / on - ly} a day a -
B♭maj7/F
Gm7(add4)
way!

from THE FANTASTICKS

Try To Remember

Words by Tom Jones
Music by Harvey Schmidt

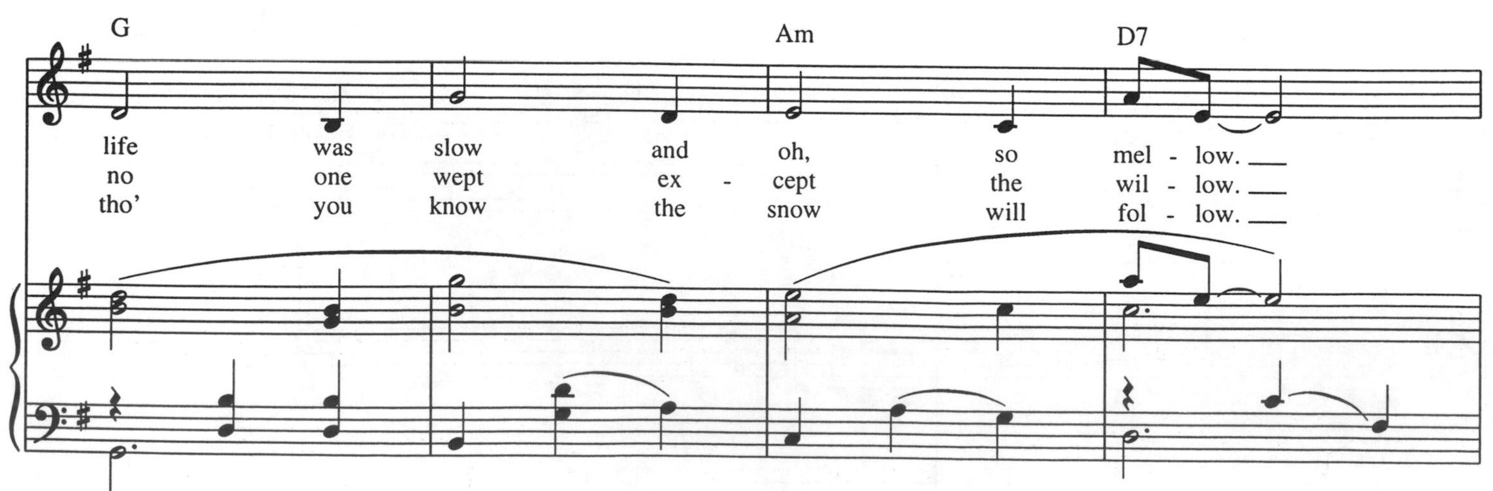

G
Am
D7
Try to re - mem - ber the kind of Sep - tem - ber when
Try to re - mem - ber when life was so ten - der that
Deep in De - cem - ber it's nice to re - mem - ber with -
G
Am
D7
grass was green and grain was yel - low.
dreams were kept be - side your pil - low.
out a hurt the heart is hol - low.
Bm7
Em7
Am7
D7
Try to re - mem - ber the kind of Sep - tem - ber when
Try to re - mem - ber when life was so ten - der that
Deep in De - cem - ber, it's nice to re - mem - ber the
mf
Gmaj7
Cmaj7
F
D7
you were a ten - der and cal - low fel - low.
love was an em - ber a - bout to bil - low.
fire of Sep - tem - ber that made us mel - low.

G
Am
D7
Try to re - mem - ber and if you re - mem - ber, then
Try to re - mem - ber and if you re - mem - ber, then
Deep in De - cem - ber our hearts should re - mem - ber and
p
1, 2
G
Cmaj7
fol - low.
fol - low.
D7
3
G
fol - low.
Cmaj7
D7
opt. G
fol - low.
rit. e decresc.
8va
pp

from NINE

Unusual Way (In A Very Unusual Way)

Words and Music by Maury Yeston

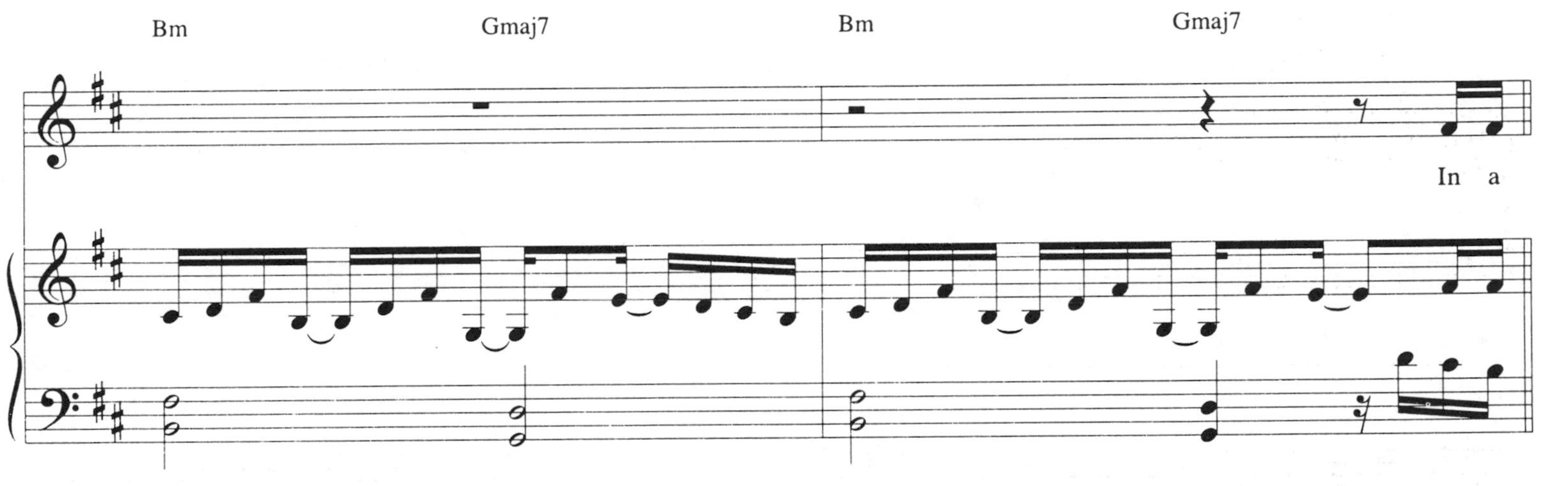

* Recorded a half step lower.

Em
Em/D
A/C♯
D
D/C♯
F♯/C♯
3
very-y un-u - su-al way___ you were my friend.
very-y un-u - su-al way___ I want to cry.

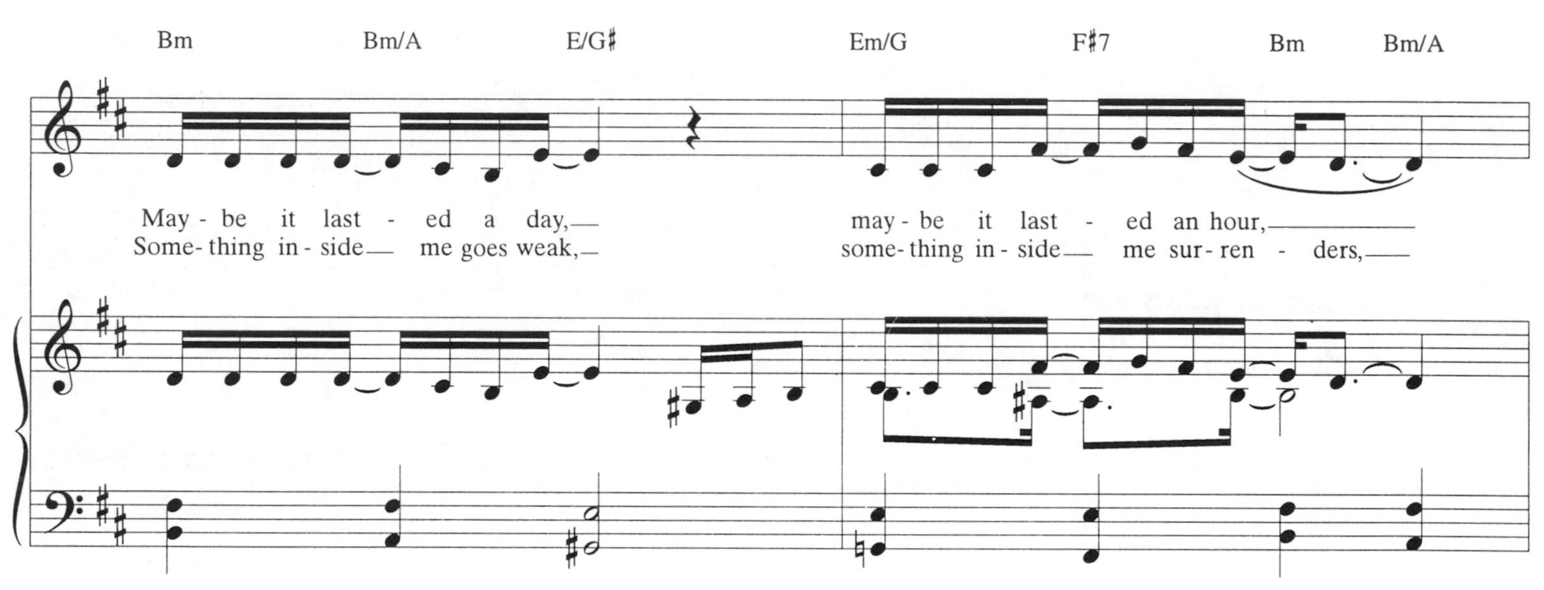
Bm
Bm/A
E/G♯
Em/G
F♯7
Bm
Bm/A
May-be it last - ed a day,___ may-be it last - ed an hour,___
Some-thing in-side___ me goes weak,___ some-thing in-side___ me sur-ren - ders,___

1.
G
C
Am7/D
Gsus4
F♯
but some-how it will nev - er end.___ In a

G Csus4 Dsus4 Bm

and you're the rea - son why___ you're the rea - son

cresc.

E/F♯ E/F♯ D♯m7/F♯

why. You don't___ know___ what you do to me;

mf

E/F♯ D♯m7/F♯ E/F♯ D♯m7/F♯

you don't___ have a clue.___ You can't___ tell___ what it's like to be

E/F♯ D♯m7/F♯ C♯m7 B/D♯ C♯m7

me, look-ing at you. It scares me so___ that I can hard - ly

F♯7sus4
speak.
Bm F♯/C♯ Bm/D B/D♯
In a ver-y un-u-su-al way — I owe what I
mp
Em Em/F♯
am to you.
Em Em/D A/C♯
Though at times it ap-pears — I won't stay, I nev-er
3
D D/C♯ F♯/C♯
go.
Bm Bm/A E/G♯
Spe-cial to me — in my life —
Em/G F♯7 Bm Bm/A
since the first day — that I met — you, —
G G/B C A/C♯
how could I ev - er for-get — you once you had touched —

D
F♯/C♯
— my soul? In — a
Bm
Bm/A
E/G♯
Em/G
F♯sus4
ver-y un-u-su-al way — you've made — me
rit.
Bm
Gmaj7
Bm
Gmaj7
whole. —
a tempo
Bm
Gmaj7
Bm
Gmaj7
Repeat and fade

from THE FULL MONTY

You Walk With Me

Words and Music by David Yazbek

D♯m G♯m C♯m F♯ B G♯m7♭5/D C♯7 F♯7
clarinet
No, not a - lone for you walk, you walk_ with me.
poco rit.
a tempo
B E7 G♯m7♭5/D C♯7 F♯7 A7 G♯m7 C♯7 F♯7
Is it the wind there o - ver my shoul-der?
A+/G G♯m7 C♯ F♯ B/D A E G♯m7 C♯
Is it your voice call - ing qui - et - ly? O - ver the hill - top, down in the val - ley,
A7 G♯m7 C♯7 F♯7 B E G♯m7♭5/D C♯7 F♯7
nev - er a - lone for you walk_ with me. When eve-ning falls
poco rit.
a tempo

*Sing the top line melody in this section for a solo version of the song.

A+/G G#m7 C#7 F# B/D A E G#m7 C#
Is it your voice call - ing qui - et - ly? O - ver the hill - top, down in the val - ley,
A7 G#m7 C#7 F#7 G#m7 B A E G#m7 C#
nev - er a - lone for you walk with me. O - ver the hill - top, down in the val - ley.
A7 G#m7 C# F#7 B E G#m7♭5/D C#7 F#7
Nev - er a - lone for you walk with me.
poco rit.
a tempo
A+/G G#m7 C# F#7 B E G#m7♭5/D C#7 F#7 B
MALCOLM:
clarinet
Nev - er a - lone for you walk with me.
rit.
a tempo
rit.

from A CHORUS LINE

What I Did For Love

Music by Marvin Hamlisch
Lyric by Edward Kleban

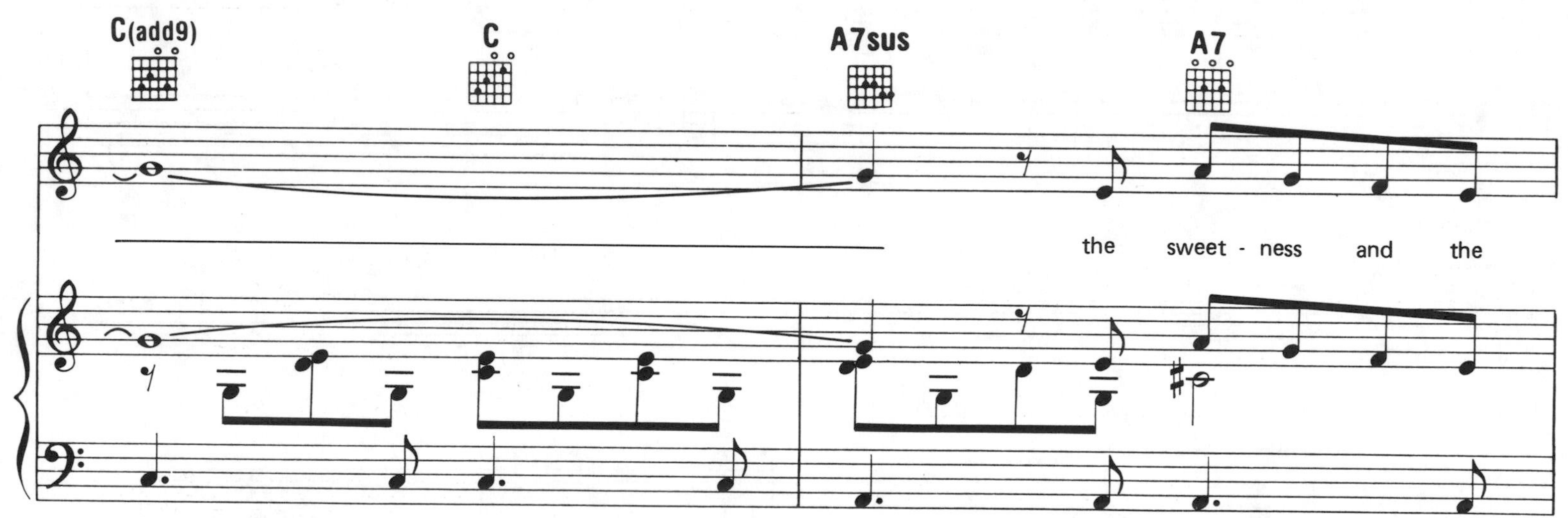

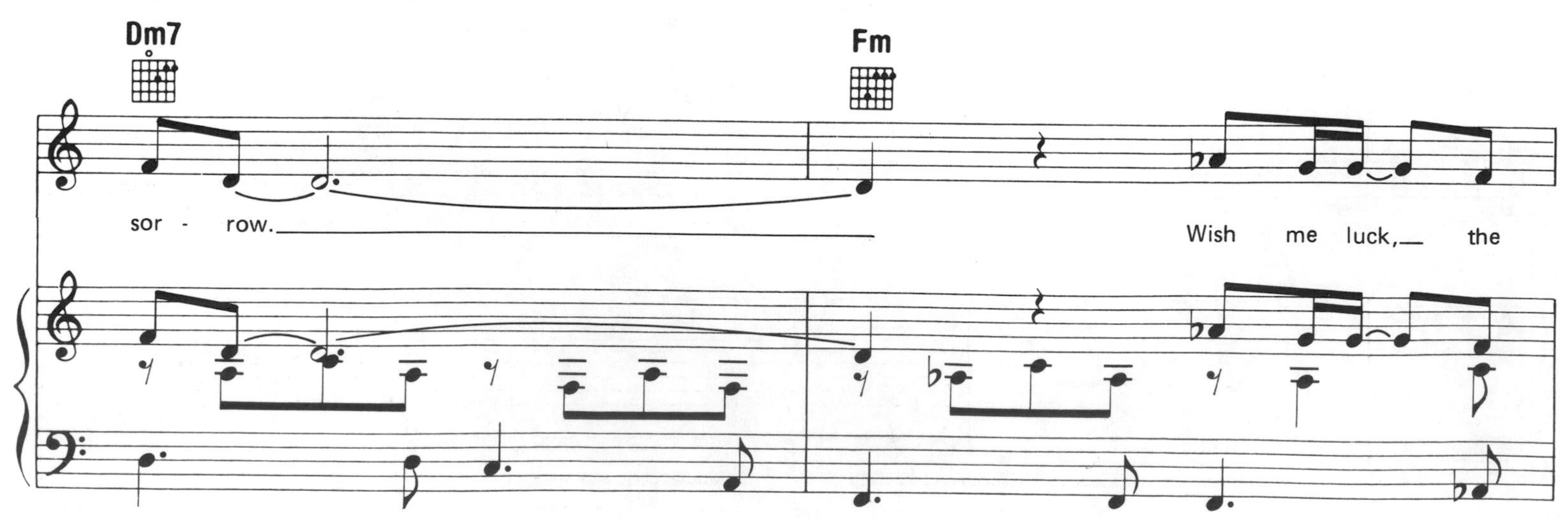

C
G/B
D9
Guitar Tacet
same to you,
But I can't re-gret
what I did for love,
what I did for
Fm
Dm7-5
G
G/F
G7
Guitar Tacet
love.
Look, my eyes are
mf
C(add9)
C
A7sus
A7
dry.
The gift was ours to

Dm7
Fm
C
G/B
bor - row.
It's as if we al - ways
D9
Guitar Tacet
Fm
knew,
And I won't for-get what I did for love,
Dm7-5
G
G/F
Em7
G/D
what I did for love.
cresc.
Am
Am/G
Fmaj7
E7sus
E7
Am
Am/G
Gone,
love is nev - er gone.
f

F#m7-5
B7sus
B7
Em
G/A
A7
As we trav - el on, love's what we'll re - mem - ber.
Dm7-5
D7sus
G7
Guitar Tacet
C(add9)
C
Kiss to-day good-bye,
mp
A7sus
A7
Dm7
and point me t'ward to - mor - row.
Fm
C
G/B
We did what we had to

Am
Am/G
D7/F♯
Am7/E
D7
do.
Won't for - get,
cresc.
F
C/E
Dm7
G7sus
G7
can't re - gret
what I did
for
C
C/B♭
Fm/A♭
Guitar Tacet
C
C/B♭
love. . .
what I did for
love
mf
Fm/A♭
Guitar Tacet
C
what I did for
love.
p
rall.
pp